PACIFIC, MO.

To John and Sally Cline

Enjoy

Pauline Masson

Pacific, Missouri

SESQUICENTENNIAL 2009

Pacific, Missouri

SESQUICENTENNIAL 2009

by
Pauline Masson

THE
DONNING COMPANY
PUBLISHERS

Pauline Masson is the author of this text. Photos not specifically attributed to other sources are also by Pauline Masson.

The Donning Company Publishers
184 Business Park Drive, Suite 206
Virginia Beach, VA 23462

Steve Mull, *General Manager*
Barbara Buchanan, *Office Manager*
Heather L. Floyd, *Editor*
Stephanie Danko, *Graphic Designer*
Derek Eley, *Imaging Artist*
Cindy Smith, *Project Research Coordinator*
Tonya Hannink, *Marketing Specialist*
Pamela Engelhard, *Marketing Advisor*

Ed Williams, *Project Director*

Library of Congress Cataloging-in-Publication Data

Masson, Pauline, 1936–
  Pacific, Missouri : sesquicentennial 2009 / by Pauline Masson.
     p. cm.
  Includes bibliographical references and index.
  ISBN 978–1–57864–609–8 (hardcover : alk. paper)
  1. Pacific (Mo.)—History. 2. Pacific (Mo.)—Centennial celebrations, etc. 3. Community life—Missouri—Pacific—History. 4. Pacific (Mo.)—Social life and customs. 5. Railroads—Missouri—Pacific—History. 6. Pacific (Mo.)—Economic conditions. I. Title.
  F474.P28M37 2010
  977.8'63—dc22

                                                                    2009052237

Printed in the United States of America at Walsworth Publishing Company

Federal, state, county, and local government officials, along with other community leaders, break ground for the $7-million project that will change the entrance to Pacific. *Photo by the author.*

Contents

Prologue

A Dot on the Map

In 1845, Capt. John C. Fremont (later general), known in history as the great Pathfinder, drew a series of lines on a map of his old surveys of the western United States, setting down his dream of a railroad from St. Louis to San Francisco. The route, which extended from St. Louis to Springfield through Rolla, would enter Franklin County nine years later at present-day Pacific.

Railroads had been carrying passengers and freight between cities on the eastern seaboard for fifteen years, but there was no railroad bridge across the Mississippi River and no railroads had been built west of the Mississippi. In Boston, railroad magnates, also looking west, called for a railroad to the Pacific Ocean. They published a flowery pamphlet extolling its benefits:

> The iron will of the sovereign people, pointing to the imperative necessity of the immediate completion of the St. Louis and San Francisco Railroad, a work whose very existence will give us the mastery of the Pacific and the India seas, thereby averting foreign wars by warning foreign powers of the necessity of being on good terms with so powerful a country as ours; a work whose very existence will ward off Indian wars… enable us to carry the mail and transmit telegraphic intelligence… and will furnish a great mart in Oregon and California for the agricultural products of the Mississippi Valley…

The dot on the map that later became Pacific lay in the path of progress.

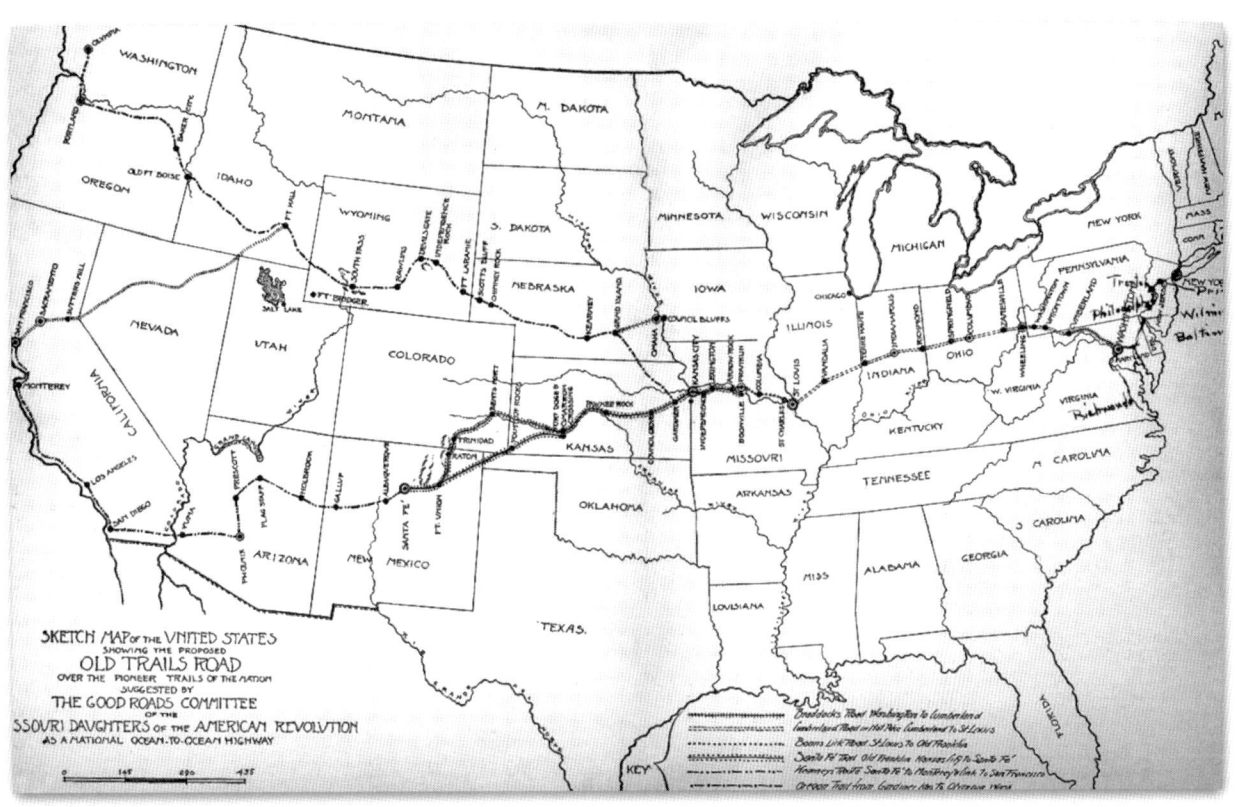

TOP: This 1911 map was created by the Good Roads Committee of the Missouri Daughters of the American Revolution. It advocated for an intercontinental highway connection between the Cumberland Trail in the East and the old Western trails, including those of John C. Fremont. *Map from the Federal Highway Administration Highway History Web page*.

ABOVE LEFT: John C. Fremont. *Photo from Wikipedia, the free encyclopedia*.

ABOVE RIGHT: Thomas Hart Benton. *Photo from Wikipedia, the free encyclopedia*.

Introduction

The spring of 2009 found the City of Pacific, Missouri, where it had always been: in a favored place.

The city was chartered in 1859 but had sprung up as a farming settlement in the preceding decades in the valley where the Meramec River loops north and all but kisses the white silica sand bluffs that have served as the city's landmark for five generations.

The Osage Indians camped along the river and on the silica escarpment, leaving enough arrowheads and other stone tools to supply generations of collectors and inspire names for streets and subdivisions. An Indian would become the school district mascot and Pacific Indians the name of district athletic teams.

The Iron Road that carried raw ore from St. James to St. Louis followed the Indian trails through this place, which was a neighbor to the surrounding communities of Fox Creek, Allenton, and Port William, where early residents picked up their mail.

One of the earliest buildings that began to give the place an identity was a simple hostelry, or inn, on the Allenton Road built by Thomas Watson. The building, which later became known as Buzzard's Roost, still exists. It is perched on a high spot at the corner of Second and Osage streets. A fading carved turkey buzzard occupies a stump in the front yard, which has faced Osage since the house was remodeled in the 1930s and the entrance moved to face the new Highway 66.

When the Pacific Railroad chose the same path as the old Iron Road for its grand scheme to build a railroad to the Pacific Ocean, it threaded its rails along the firmest part of the shelf between the river and the bluff.

Pacific City Hall at 300 Hoven Drive is the government center, housing the mayor's office, administration offices, city collector, and city police department.

John C. Fremont, the famous Pathfinder, had chosen this route for a railroad to the Pacific Ocean as early as the 1840s. Fremont and Missouri Senator Thomas Hart Benton secured the financing for a railroad from St. Louis to the Pacific and began construction on July 1, 1851.

In anticipation of the railroad, William Inks platted a small town around the junction where Fremont's two planned railroads would split. He called it Franklin, in honor of Benjamin Franklin, echoing the name of the county. Inks' plat included a spot for the railroad depot, which was hastily constructed in readiness for the first train.

The first steam train excursion west of the Mississippi River delivered its passengers to Franklin (Pacific) on July 23, 1853.

After some discussion about another town named Franklin, the town fathers changed the name of the new city to Pacific, forever solidifying its ties to the railroad.

For the next seventy years, Pacific enjoyed a commercial and industrial boom fed by the dozens of passenger and freight trains that served the city each day. As a result of the national railroad shopmen's strike in 1922, the Missouri Pacific Railroad closed the repair shops in Pacific, ending the economic boom—and one by one, the factories and mills disappeared and the stores closed.

Eighty years after the strike, the city paused to reassess its railroad history and took a lasting look at the eighty or more freight and Amtrak trains that passed through the city every day. Forward-thinking leaders adopted the railroad as a brand or theme around which to create a tourism promotion plan. A group of civic leaders began to develop a miniature park, named Pacific Station Plaza, as a train-watching venue on South First Street near the site of the former train station.

The cover photo depicts the arrival of Frisco Engine 1522, which stopped in Pacific on its final run as a salute to the Pacific railroad heritage, commemorating the arrival of the first passenger train that had arrived in Pacific 150 years earlier.

Today the city is reinventing itself as a place to visit, live, and do business. Citizen committees studied the city's sesquicentennial, tourism, and transportation prospects. Civic and service groups have established informal agreements to use their combined strengths and skills to show the city in its best light.

Signs located at the city entrance on East and West Osage, Historic Route 66, welcome motorists to Pacific. The Pacific Rotary Club erected the signs.

Sand Mountain, on Historic Route 66, is the city's most prominent landmark. Blackburn Park, atop the bluff, offers a spectacular view of the city and the Meramec Valley beyond.

FROM THE *Mayor*

$\mathcal{I}$t's not an easy thing to single out one element of our city and say this is what we're all about in Pacific.

Our location has certainly favored us over the years, giving us natural deposits of sand and gravel in the sand bluffs and the river. It was no accident that the builders of a great railroad chose this place for their route west and southwest. This is the ideal valley between the Missouri River and Meramec River.

Today, our location as the entrance city to Franklin County and occupying part of St. Louis County is still serving our city. The Missouri Department of Transportation is currently rebuilding the entrance to Pacific. They're widening Interstate 44 from our doorstep to the Highway 100 exit that leads to Washington, Missouri.

Pacific is partnering with MoDOT to create a pedestrian pathway beneath the I-44 overpass, connecting the hotel on the north side to restaurants and a future shopping district on the south side of the interstate.

This past year, our city went through what some of our citizens see as its finest hour. That, too, was a result of our location. The Meramec River left its banks in March 2008, inundating 180 homes and thirty-six businesses. Our citizens and neighbors poured into the south side ahead of the rising water, helping residents to move their belongings to safety. Our city staff made arrangements for them to store their

Mayor Herbert Adams, left, chats with Secretary of State Robin Carnahan and Pacific resident Sterling Hearns.

belongings safely and free of charge until they could get back into their homes or find new homes.

Our city staff spent the next 400 days working to find assistance for the flood victims. On May 19, 2009, I signed the purchase contract to use FEMA/SEMA funds to purchase the first home in a twenty-seven-home flood buyout. We're still working to find financial assistance to elevate the remaining homes above the one-hundred-year flood level.

One of the most rewarding aspects of our city today is that builders have bought up lots in the flooded area and built the new, elevated homes in our oldest neighborhood—something not seen for half a century.

Sesquicentennial Committee
Former mayor Jeffrey Titter, looking ahead, requested the formation of a citywide sesquicentennial celebration recognizing the city's 150th birthday. Mayor Herbert Adams agreed that the city would host a series of events if Mr. Titter would chair a committee. After Mr. Titter's marriage in 2008, Michelle Bruns stepped in to complete the celebration. Committee members seated from the left are Keith Bruns, vice chairman; Michelle Bruns, chairman; and Jeannie Bandermann, secretary. Standing from the left are Terry Steelman, Debbie Kelley, Jim Schwinkendorf, Hilda Bandermann, Ruth Muehler, and Nellie Mueller. Not pictured are Dee Walton, Dennis Oliver, Rosalind Jordan, and Jeffrey Titter.

Which brings me to another element of our city that defines it. Our people.

We disagree often, and sometimes loudly, which I happen to believe is a healthy thing, but our citizens today are participating in a dozen different committees to make Pacific a better place.

Members of these committees are working to improve our parks and cemeteries, support our schools, encourage economic development, attract tourists, and plan a grand celebration marking our sesquicentennial year.

As mayor, I appointed the Sesquicentennial Committee at the request of former mayor Jeffrey Titter. I asked Mayor Titter to chair the committee and he agreed, but happily, he was married in 2008 and moved out of the city. Michelle Bruns stepped in to spearhead the work of the committee. She has done an outstanding job, overseeing a 150th birthday parade, a "settler's style" community picnic, construction of a Sesquicentennial Pavilion in Liberty Field, an interfaith Hymn Sing at the Presbyterian Church, a concluding ceremony at our annual Railroad Day celebration in September, and the compilation of this book.

I'm especially proud of the first 150 years of our city's history and the people who are striving to assure that we live up to our potential during the next 150 years.

Respectfully,
Mayor Herbert Adams

GOVERNMENT BY THE *People*

*P*acific is a fourth-class city of approximately 7,000 people, which is run by a mayor, elected at large. He is supported by a city administrator, community and economic development director, city clerk, city engineer, and city attorney.

Six aldermen represent constituents in three city wards. Aldermen serve on administrative and public works committees to review complex matters before they are presented for board action.

The city has approximately fifty paid employees. The Public Works Department maintains the city-owned water works, sewer system, and roads and bridges. The Building Department performs inspections and issues construction permits.

A seven-member Planning and Zoning Commission reviews all building and development plans and makes a recommendation to the Board of Aldermen.

Another ninety civic-minded citizens serve on boards, commissions, and committees to help run city parks, cemeteries, and a historic museum. A city Industrial Development Authority administers a low-interest municipal bond financing program to firms that improve the city's economy. A Tourism Committee oversees the spending of voter-approved tourism tax funds. A Board of Adjustment litigates disputes between property owners and the city building codes. Following the 2008 flood, an emergency management committee reviewed the city's preparedness and response to the disaster and issued a report to the mayor.

City aldermen wholeheartedly approved the Sesquicentennial Committee's efforts. Above they are Mike Bates, Ward 1; Walter Arnette, Ward 2; Dave Monroe, Ward 1; Jerry Eversmeyer, Ward 2; Carol Johnson, Ward 2; and Mike Pigg, Ward 3.

Harold Selby, city administrator.

Kim Barfield, city clerk.

Sheila Steelman, community and economic development director.

Debbie Kelley, city collector.

Ron Reed, municipal court judge.

An additional fifty or so individuals volunteer their time in civic organizations that run parades, competitions, and other community celebrations.

The city has its own police department, which is overseen by an elected police chief. This department participates in the Franklin County Drug Task Force. The city is served by the Pacific Fire Protection District, which is headquartered in the city, and by the Meramec Ambulance District, headquartered in Villa Ridge with an ambulance station in Pacific.

The Board of Adjustment members are Bill Devine, Bob Kalin, Terry Steelman, Ronald Suerig, Gayle Rogan, and alternate Dan McClain.

The Planning and Zoning Commission members are Linda Bruns (chairman), Jim Smith (vice chairman), Bob Sanders, Thomas E. Miles, Gary Koelling, Gary Bay, Josh Grodie, Barbara Sacco, and Mike Bates.

The Park Board members are Joe Mueller (president), Stephen Flannery III (vice president), Curtis Bates, Mary Hoven, Sarah Faszold, Thomas E. Miles, and Tina Bell.

The Cemetery Committee members are Ruth Muehler, Harlan Bruns, Laura Noonan, Emma Moore, Jeanne Groth, Kay LeClaire, Bob Myers, Edith McLaren, and Mike Pigg.

The city also operates a municipal court, which acts on traffic violations and violations of city ordinances. Ron Reed, who served as police chief for twenty-five years, was elected municipal judge in 2006. He is assisted by Nina Weatherspoon, court clerk, and Mary Wideman, deputy court clerk.

The Meramec Valley Historical Museum Committee members are Hilda Bandermann

The City Hall staff seated from the left are Daphne Lindemann, billing, and Janet Fuszner, accounts payable clerk. Standing from the left are Mary Wideman, treasurer, and Nina Weatherspoon, court clerk.

The Building Department members are Glenda Titter, deputy city clerk; Bill Davis, inspector; Dave Myers, building commissioner; and Richard Adams, inspector and animal control.

Jim Brune, Pacific police chief.

The Pacific police officers front from the left are Officer Tracy Riegel, Officer Shelly Young, Officer Dian Becker, Officer Sara Young, and Officer Carrie Moore. Center from the left are Cpt. Mark Becker, Officer Chris Keil, administrative assistant Angela Downing, Officer Andrew Whitman, Officer Cynthia Garner, Officer Tony Davis, Sgt. Dan Donnelly, Officer Roy Anderson, Officer Scott Perkins, Officer Art Tullock, Sgt. Cal Callaway, Officer Nelvin Cawley, and Cpl. Detective Larry Cook. Back from the left are Officer Rodney Backues, Officer Harvey Nowak, Officer Jeremy Lynn, Officer Matt Garrecht, and Officer Don Locke.

(president), Ruth Muehler (vice president), Jeannie Bandermann (secretary), Donna McMullin (treasurer), Janet Daniel (curator), Edith McLaren, Jeffrey Titter, and Alderman Jerry Eversmeyer. Volunteers are Peggy Bolar, Laura Noonan, Therissa Schlemper, Ginger Gallagher, Ron Sansone, Loyd Harris, Kay LeClaire, and Duke Matlock.

The Industrial Development Authority members are William Rutledge (chairman), Bob Schneider, Keith Bruns, Dennis Oliver, and Dale Glass.

The Tourism Committee members are Tim Baker (chairman), Brad Reed, Andy Patel, John Behrer, Betty Cochran, and Walter Arnette.

The Building Department Advisory Board members are Dave Myers, Bill Davis, Fire Chief Rick Friedmann, Deputy Fire Chief Kenny Prichard, Linda Bruns, Josh Grodie, Phil Hovey, Ed Gass, and Nick Sacco. The liaisons are Josiah Holst, Mike Pigg, Mayor Herb Adams, and City Administrator Harold Selby.

The City Public Works Department personnel from the left are Roy Hinkle, Darrell Boyer, Larry Bingaman, Ben Boedges, Stephen Woodruff, Robert Vancil, Donald Dailey, Robert Lefarth, Robert Brueggemann, Charlie Love, and Joe Emory.

The Pacific Fire District operates three stations, serving areas in Franklin, Jefferson, and St. Louis counties. Fire District officers pictured from the left are Fire Chief Rick Friedmann, Deputy Chief Kenny Prichard, Captain Stan Pursley, Captain Robert Willoughby, Inspector Jim Briesacher, Lieutenant Dustin Wagner, Battalion Chief Gary Graf, Battalion Chief Scott Friedmann, and Firefighter/Engineer Tom Grgic.

The Emergency Management Advisory Committee members are Bob Masson (chairman), Dave Myers, Fire Chief Rick Friedmann, Ambulance District Chief Christine Neal, Sheila Steelman, Tracy Maher, Genetta Tomnitz, Sergeant Dan Donnelly, Angela Downing, Reverend Dan Stratmann, Carol Johnson, and City Administrator Harold Selby.

The Road and Bridge Committee members are Ed Bruns (chairman), Pauline Masson (vice chairman), Fire Chief Rick Friedmann, Ambulance District Chief Christine Neal, Elaine Brune, Police Chief Jim Brune, and Alderman Jerry Eversmeyer. School Superintendent Randy George, Paul Marquart, Bill Devine Jr., and Reverend Kenneth Lawson are citizen members. Alternates are Mayor Herb Adams, City Administrator Harold Selby, and Presiding Commissioner Ed Hillhouse.

Pacific is served by the Meramec Ambulance District, which maintains a station on East Osage.

Preface

The little farm community tucked into the corner of the Meramec River Valley where three counties come together received its first jolt of travel excitement around 1847. A farmer returning from St. Louis had important news. Two steamboats were on their way to the Moselle Iron Works and would pass by on the Meramec River. The news was carried from house to house. Anticipation was so keen that a large gathering assembled on the bluff near the Dr. Jeffries farm to see for themselves if paddlewheel steamers could navigate the Meramec.

The shrill whistle in the distance was followed by graceful curves of smoke around the hills. The sound of powerful engines and splash of the paddle wheel followed. As they passed by, the spectators could read the names, *The Petrel* and the *Dove*. They moved on upriver to the Moselle Iron Works where they loaded with iron and waited for a rain. Then, they started downstream. *The Petrel* was in the lead. She ran safely past the place but the *Dove* had been delayed and the river was falling. The men on board threw off some iron, near where the fish trap was made twenty years earlier. Again she started downriver and again lodged and was aground about a mile below town. There she waited nearly a year for a heavy rain, then was run a few miles farther down before she turned across the stream and was broken in two and destroyed.

The neighborhood was not treated to any more sensations of importance until the building of the railroad.

Anonymous

A horse and buggy on the road that led up Prospect Hill before construction of Route 66 carved away part of the hill, leaving the bluff that we see today. *From the MVG&HS collection*.

Meramec RIVER

*F*rench explorers looking for ore entered the Meramec River from the Mississippi in the 1700s. Some explorers founded the French settlement of St. Genevieve to the south, but not enough ore was found in this region to sustain a settlement.

The Meramec Valley, with its high bluffs, craggy woodlands, and occasional prairies, became a haven for settlers. Unlike the prairies north of the Missouri River that easily opened up wagon trails, the Meramec Valley was compact and rugged, requiring settlers to stake out paths along steep slopes.

One particular group of settlers looking for cheap land and a refuge from the xenophobia in St. Louis found safety in the inaccessible valleys. Irish immigrants made their way to the LaBarque Creek from the Meramec in the early 1800s.

From its headwaters on the southwest slope of Signal Hill to its terminus in the Meramec River opposite Allenton, the five-mile long LaBarque Creek drains a rugged irregular section of the Ozarks. This section comprises about eighteen square miles, mostly hills of various altitudes, "enclosing winding valleys as irregular as are the hills," according to Joseph McNamee (1864–1950), teacher, author, and lifelong resident of the hills.

Around 1800, a group of Irish immigrants, seeking a place to be free of discrimination, made their way up the Meramec to the mouth of LaBarque Creek, south of present-day Pacific.

"There are many peaks, high ridges, and level plateaus, broken by gaps or passes, and here and there small patches of bare sand rock," McNamee wrote circa 1945. "However… there are probably four or five square miles of level land between the Meramec and the high bluffs, and numerous narrow level valleys among the various ranges of hills."

Today, a group calling themselves the LaBarque Creek Stakeholders are a mix of fifth-generation property owners (including some McNamee descendants), commuters who have built architectural jewels in hidden clearings, and self-proclaimed nature lovers who want to keep the rugged area in its native state.

Steamboat travel never worked out on the shallow Meramec River, but the river was a passageway to the little valley beside the white bluffs and beyond to the vast timber fields in the extreme northeast corner of the Ozark uplift. The Irish Catholics would build a log church in 1848 on "the right bank" of the Meramec, a stone's throw from present-day Pacific.

In the late 1820s and 1830s, a handful of houses were built in present-day Pacific. In 1833, Nelson Withington built a house in what is now the City of Pacific. The house has not survived but Thomas Watson built a house in 1854, later called Buzzard's Roost, that still stands.

Early roads leading to the little farm-to-market hamlet were the Allenton road to the east, Gray Summit to the north, and Little Ireland road to the south. Settlers made the trip to Port William, present-day Gray Summit, to pick up what mail they received. This was the frontier, remote and rugged.

The industrious farmers cut timber to clear the land and planted corn and wheat crops and kitchen gardens. Cash could be made by selling pelts to eager buyers who made their way up the river. In the 1840s and 1850s, beaver pelts would bring extra income to farm families.

The settlers erected a wooden bridge over the Meramec River as early as 1870, allowing commerce between the residents at the foot of the bluff and those in Little Ireland.

The settlers soon learned that the Meramec could be a volatile neighbor, overflowing its banks and inundating the lowlands. When

Commerce between settlers on both sides of the Meramec began early and bridges, like the covered bridge above, were built across the river. *From the MVG&HS collection.*

The Meramec River is a recreational waterway when it is at peace.

heavy ice melts from the north swelled the Mississippi, floodwaters pushed up the Meramec Valley all the way to its headwaters. Heavy spring rains in the steep Ozark watershed to the south could pour into the Meramec, sending a two-mile wide overflow covering farmlands all the way to its mouth. The craggy tributaries—Fox Creek, LaBarque Creek, Brush Creek, and Wade Creek—were equally perilous, pouring their runoff water into the Meramec like milk pouring from a pitcher.

Geologists describe a one-hundred-year flood as a flood that would happen only once in one hundred years, but the name is misleading. Fed by a treacherous watershed, the present-day Pacific would see the dreaded one-hundred-year floods in 1850, 1915, 1982, 1994, 2002, and 2008.

The south side of Pacific was inundated in the flood of 1982. *From the MVG&HS collection.*

Mayor Herbert Adams vowed that the 2008 flood would be the last crippling flood.

The flood of 2008 inundated 180 homes and thirty-six businesses in Old Town Pacific, but as modern reporting procedures gave south side residents early warning, city officials and residents responded with a massive support system.

South First Street was flooded as far north as the McHugh-Dailey Building during the flood of 1915.

City police officers went door to door to warn people of rising water. An Emergency Operations Center (EOC) was set up in the meeting room at City Hall and a shelter for victims was set up at Riverbend School. Street crews began to close off streets to traffic. Volunteers showed up to help residents move furniture and belongings out of harm's way. Other volunteers began to collect cleaning supplies for victims, which were delivered to City Hall.

Sheila Steelman, the city's community and economic development director of eight years, found businesses in the industrial parks that allowed residents to store their belongings free of charge.

The Building Department also began going door to door, making sure everyone was out—and posting buildings with a process to be followed that would allow them to return.

Volunteers filled sand bags and stacked them around the McHugh-Dailey Building at First and Orleans streets and the historic building that houses Osage

Realty across the street. Although the floodwater would rise to Orleans Street, both those buildings were protected.

As the waters receded, Service International, a faith-based flood recovery organization, came to the city and offered to clean up the flood damage at no cost to anyone.

As the clean-up was going on, city fathers began to explore the Federal Emergency Management Authority (FEMA) and State Emergency Management Authority (SEMA) flood buyout program. The city was awarded a grant to buy out twenty-seven homes located directly in the floodway and turn the residential lots into permanent green space.

Some homeowners in the adjoining floodplain used their insurance company offer to elevate their homes above the one-hundred-year flood level. City leaders are seeking funds to elevate the remaining homes.

Private builders saw opportunities on the south side and began buying up lots and abandoned homes. They have constructed a series of new, affordable, single-family homes in Old Town.

The sesquicentennial year found Old Town Pacific in a renaissance. On St. Louis Street, one block north of the railroad tracks, property owners are restoring the 1870s brick storefront residential buildings.

The Pacific Partnership, founded in 2002 to revitalize the city's first neighborhood and business district, looked at the eighty or more trains a day that travel through the city, adopted a former city maintenance yard south of the tracks, and began the development of Pacific Station Plaza as a public mini-park where visitors could watch the trains that still whiz through the city.

Today, Pacific is a river town and a railroad town as never before. The city has edged away from the river but maintained its spot in the Meramec Valley. At the same time, the city has staked out its ownership in its railroad heritage. ✑

Mayor Herb Adams signs the first contract to buy the homes on the south side and turn the land into green space like the vacant lot below.

Houses that are bought out will be demolished and the lots will be seeded and planted, creating green spaces like this south side lot.

A view of downtown Pacific during the flood of March 2008.

Railroad ARRIVES

The tail end of the summer of 1853 was filled with excitement.

It was reported that a railroad was to be built, but none of the farmers knew where the location would be. This gave an opportunity for speculators to purchase the farms. William C. Inks purchased the Watson Farm. James H. Morley bought the Lollar farm. T. M. Alt purchased the farm of Leonard Reed, and Blumenthal bought the Johnson farm.

In 1851, Inks platted the first section of the town and called it Franklin. The plat contained 256 lots. He named the streets the names they still have today, except for Adelaide Street, which was later renamed Columbus Street.

Progress of the new Pacific Railroad heading west from St. Louis brought the tracks closer to the newly platted town of Franklin. In the past, the life of the farmers had been cut off from the commerce to the east and the vast, largely unexplored territory to the west. Citizens could count on one hand the number of young men lured west by the War with Mexico or the California gold rush two years earlier. They traded their produce and their services with each other, which was a good and cheerful life. Still, they were anxious to know how soon the railroad would be coming.

In the summer of 1851, construction began on the Pacific Railroad, the first railroad built in the state, designed with the intention of making St. Louis the center of a vast rail network. On that July day, two years later, suspense mounted in Franklin as the promised first train approached.

"When it arrives, how grand the scene. Flags are waving from the cars, the engine is decked with wreaths and flags, men are waving their hats and sending

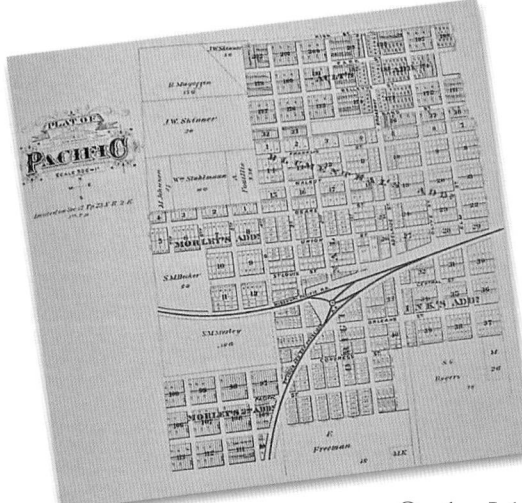

William C. Inks drew up the first official plat of Pacific. *From the MVG&HS collection.*

up cheer after cheer. Flat cars were good enough for this first ride over the new railroad. The day is spent in sightseeing. It is a good opportunity to buy lots, and some have taken advantage of it. Evening approaches and the whistle of the engine warns all concerned that they must get ready," an anonymous historian penned circa 1870.

When the steam train made the thirty-seven-mile trip from downtown St. Louis to Franklin in July 1853, it was the first steam train excursion west of the Mississippi River. Twelve flat cars carried dignitaries and sightseers to the newborn little city. The passengers detrained and looked around at the throng gathered to greet the train. Some walked down to the riverbank and made the decision to buy a lot and stay. Six years later, the town officially changed its name to Pacific, solidifying its tie to the railroad.

The presence of the railroad would give Pacific a significant importance in the Civil War. Both Union and Confederate generals eyed their military maps and pinpointed the spot where two railroads—capable of carrying troops and material—converged.

As the Missouri Tourism Department begins its statewide celebration of the 150th anniversary of Civil War in 2011, local historians also began to research military activities that took place in the town of Pacific (Franklin).

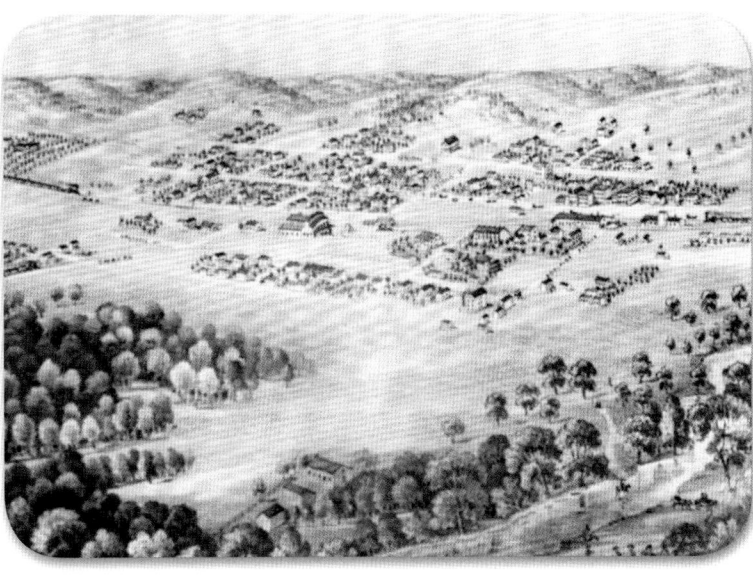

This hand-drawn map, showing the bucolic community of Pacific, was drawn and signed by A. Ruger in 1869. *From the MVG&HS collection.*

The Pacific Railroad's first locomotive, the Pacific, bore the number *3*, weighed 29,000 pounds, and cost $7,650. In July of 1853, rails extended thirty-eight miles from downtown St. Louis to Franklin. The train to make that trip was pulled by a locomotive made in the new St. Louis locomotive plant of Palm & Robertson. *From the MVG&HS collection.*

CIVIL *War* IN PACIFIC

$\mathcal{T}$he war started on April 13, 1861, when the Confederates fired on Ft. Sumter, South Carolina. Two months later, in June 1861, Pacific Postmaster William Inks was pressed into service by Union General Nathaniel Lyon, headquartered in St. Louis, to command the Pacific Battalion Home Guard, consisting of six companies and totaling 316 men, with the duties to guard the bridges of the Pacific Railroad in Franklin, Jefferson, and St. Louis counties.

In September 1861, the Home Guard was mustered out of service when Lt. Col. Francis J. Herron (later brigadier general) brought the 9th Iowa Regiment to Pacific and established Camp Herron "between two bluffs that rise in splendid magnificence… between huge rocks, enormous stumps and clumps of bushes," as one member of Herron's brigade later recorded.

Men in Herron's regiment recorded in their diaries that a malaria outbreak afflicted troops while they were stationed at Camp Herron. The sick men were taken to a hospital in Pacific. A mansion on St. Louis Street, where the Bank of America now stands, was requisitioned as an Army hospital. The house was later known as The Blue Goose.

As Christmas approached, the regiment was so comfortable in Pacific that the decision was made to celebrate. A printed invitation dated December 5, 1861, announced a Grand Union Ball given by the officers stationed at Pacific City, Missouri, organized by Col. Herron. Honorary managers included Gen. Curtis, Gen. Harding, Col. Herron, and Col. A. W. Maupin.

This former residence on St. Louis Street, known as The Blue Goose, was believed to have been used for a Civil War hospital. *From the MVG&HS collection.*

As the war in Missouri wound to what Union generals thought was the end, the railroad junction at Pacific would again pop up on military maps. In 1864, the community experienced a skirmish between Confederate and Union forces during Gen. Sterling Price's Missouri Expedition when Price, with a hastily accumulated army, advanced north from Arkansas with hopes of taking St. Louis and Jefferson City so that he could capture troops and munitions.

Price knew Missouri like the back of his hand. He had moved to the state in 1831 as a young man, living in Fayette and Keytesville and finally farming near Bowling Green. He served as the governor of Missouri from 1853 to 1857.

On September 30, Price sent generals Shelby and Marmaduke to Franklin County. Union General A. J. Smith was ordered from Illinois to Pacific to stop them. On October 1, Confederate General William Cabell and his brigade entered Pacific just after sunrise and gutted the stores and houses of valuables. They set fire to the train depot, the water tanks, the railroad shops, the public icehouse, and several railroad bridges over the Meramec. Around 10:00 a.m., Union Colonel E. H. Wolfe's brigade drove the Confederates out of town.

About sixty people in Franklin County, none in Pacific, were killed during Price's raid, according to historical records. No woman of the county is on record as being killed or hurt. Southern sympathizers were not robbed.

Price's northern advance was stopped at Pacific and diverted toward Union and Jefferson City and eventually south, back to Arkansas. For years, a large bronze plaque marked the site on present-day East Osage pinpointing the closest point that Price came to achieving his goal of reaching St. Louis. The plaque has since disappeared.

When Gen. Price raided the area in October of 1864, many of the German children looked on the general as a "Boggy Man." When word spread of the forthcoming raid by the Confederates, some of the children of one family hid under a wagon all day long in great fear. Other children had been sent by fearful families to St. Louis to stay with relatives. But, like Price, some local families still clung to their Southern dreams.

In Gray Summit, where Alice Virginia Jeffries and her family and friends lived, Gen. Price and his Confederate band were welcomed with open arms, a barbecue was prepared for Price, and a celebration was held on the lawn of the home of the Miles family, with many of the old Southern families in attendance.

When the war ended, the Pacific Railroad and the little city just inside the Franklin County line were not even in their teens. Like a rambunctious twelve-year-old, they were eager to grow.

LEFT: Colonel Francis J. Herron. *Photo from the Missouri Civil War Heritage Foundation.*

RIGHT: General Sterling Price. *Photo from the Missouri Civil War Heritage Foundation.*

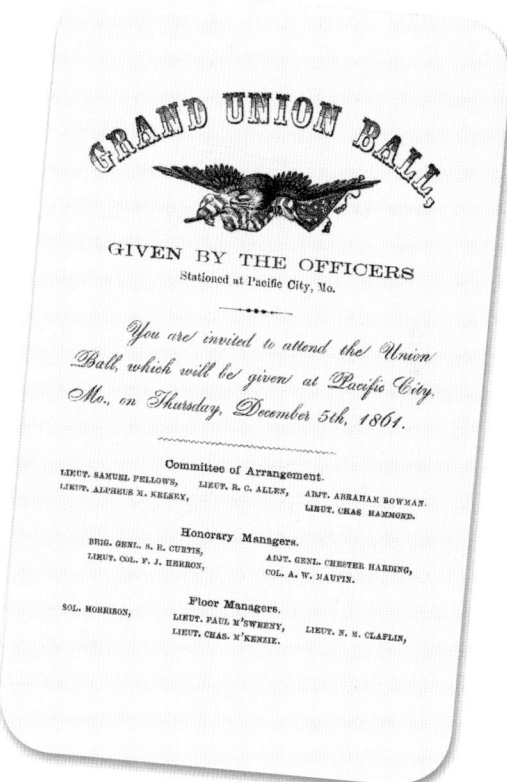

An invitation to the 1861 Grand Union Ball in Pacific. *Photo from the Missouri Civil War Heritage Foundation.*

RAILROAD *Boom* YEARS

*I*n the seventy years following the Civil War, the plat that Inks had drawn near the railroad tracks would fill in with houses and businesses, some which would be operated by the same families for three generations.

In the early 1870s, the Missouri Pacific Railroad further blessed the community when Robert Peck, building and bridge superintendent, moved his headquarters from Washington to Pacific at the junction of the two railroads. He constructed a turntable, roundhouse with three stalls, blacksmith, and engine repair shop in Pacific. He also established his bridge works here, which employed 1,000 men.

During that decade, rows of brick storefronts went up on St. Louis Street. Some are still occupied today in what has become Old Town Pacific. Recent improvement completely rebuilt First Street and St. Louis Street, adding vintage electric lights and a vintage clock.

Those decades, which would become known as the Golden Age of Railroading, transformed the gritty little farm community. The provincials, who could be drawn to the riverbank with the promise of seeing a steamboat on the Meramec, emerged as a community of well-traveled citizens who built a fine schoolhouse and a host of churches and carried on a longstanding romance with the growing number of trains that stopped there each day.

During those years, the railroad defined the community. There are few cities in the United States where the city was actually named after a railroad, as opposed to the other way around. But with the City of Pacific, that is what happened. The community of Franklin was renamed Pacific, Missouri, in 1859 to recognize the importance of the arrival of the railroad in town. The Pacific Railroad was chartered by the State of Missouri in 1849 to extend "from St. Louis to the western boundary of Missouri and thence to the Pacific Ocean." Groundbreaking began in St. Louis on July 4, 1851, with construction progressing westward. The first train didn't arrive in Franklin until July of 1853, following completion of a pair of tunnels at Barrett (now Kirkwood). That segment of the Pacific Railroad construction continued westward, finally arriving at Washington in February of 1855, due to encountering some financial problems. These tracks later became the main line of the Missouri Pacific Railroad, and today is a heavily traveled line of the Union Pacific Railroad.

In 1852, construction of the Southwest Branch of the Pacific Railroad was authorized. This line started at Franklin and was completed to Rolla in 1861. It became the Southwest Pacific Railroad, and later became the main line of the St. Louis-San Francisco Railway, known as the Frisco. Today, it is a part of Burlington Northern Santa Fe Railway (BNSF).

The history of railroad companies and their ownership is complicated, and changed from one entrepreneur to another a number of times. Financial difficulties caused several changes in ownership, but by the late 1860s and early 1870s, the two lines in Pacific had become established as the Missouri Pacific (MP) and the Frisco (SLSF) railroads. The Frisco entered St. Louis from Pacific over the Missouri Pacific tracks until it constructed its own line in 1883.

In 1871, the MP built a freight car repair facility in Pacific in the vicinity of today's commuter parking lot, just south of the old downtown area. A turntable was also installed to turn the steam engines of both railroads and a three-stall

TOP AND BOTTOM: As the heyday of passenger rail service in the U.S. flourished, downtown Pacific was a busy mercantile center. Mauthe's Department Store was built in 1870 and continued in business for a little over one hundred years. Hotels, restaurants, and saloons were sandwiched between retail stores. *From the MVG&HS collection.*

The Pacific Depot sat between the two sets of railroad tracks, east of South First and St. Louis streets, approximately where Adelaide (later Columbus) Street reached the tracks. The stately brick building served both the Pacific and Frisco railroads. After regular passenger service was discontinued, it was demolished. *From the MVG&HS collection.*

St. Louis Street was the city retail center circa 1915. *From the MVG&HS collection.*

In this often-reprinted view of Pacific from the bluff in Blackburn Park, the careful observer can see the row of buildings that housed the railroad shops beyond the line of trees. *From the MVG&HS collection.*

roundhouse was built. Pacific had a substantial brick passenger station that was used by both railroads. Due to the rolling hills in the area, Pacific was an important stop for steam engines to replenish their water supplies. Both railroads had a number of large water tanks to quench the hungry thirsts of the steamers.

During the three decades from 1870 to 1900, some 150 new businesses were established in the immediate area of the railroad depot, including the Missouri Pacific car shops, which occupied a dozen buildings in its heyday.

Among the new businesses were nine hotels, half a dozen general merchandise stores, three butchers, four grocers, four barbers, a tannery, three shoemakers, a feed store, and a dozen saloons. There were also the occasional dentist, jeweler, tailor, and tin shop. A few blocks from the commercial center, two roller mills, two blacksmith shops, two wagon builders, a brickyard, half a dozen sand and gravel companies, and a marble cutter could be found.

The *Franklin County Democrat* began publishing a newspaper in Pacific in 1871, followed by *Our County Paper* in 1883 and the *Pacific Transcript* in 1891. The *Transcript* would continue to publish until 1985. The *Transcript* was the quintessential hometown newspaper, reporting family visits, train schedules, and train injuries. A February 15,

As the Boston Railroad magnates had predicted, the railroad provided markets for Pacific products. Banner Roller Mills dominated the downtown skyline and is also visible in the photo above. *From the MVG&HS collection.*

The giant milking barn at Beauchamp's Dairy delivered milk to the St. Louis School District, and in its heyday to every commercial dairy in the city of St. Louis. *From the MVG&HS collection.*

1916 article promoting safety when crossing the tracks reminded citizens that a train traveling sixty miles per hour was covering 5,280 feet per minute, or eighty-eight feet per second.

The merchants built for themselves a series of substantial homes both brick and frame. A row of fine Victorian homes was built on Adelaide Street, also known as Silk Stocking Row, which on October 20, 1892, changed to Columbus Avenue to commemorate the 400th anniversary of the discovery of America by Columbus.

In September 1894, W. E. Bailey started the Pacific Electric Company and was granted permission to erect buildings, apparatus, a steam plant, and put up poles and wires to supply the City of Pacific and its inhabitants with electric lights and motor power.

The new company was given permission to enter any street, alley, avenue, bridge, or public grounds. The agreement was to continue for twenty years. The flat rate for residential electric service was one dollar a month. The following January, the company entered into an agreement to put up twenty streetlights for a cost of one dollar and fifty cents a month for each light. Lights were placed on Franklin, Walnut, Columbus, Osage, Seventh, Fifth, First, Union at Sixth, Fourth, Second and Columbus, St. Louis Street at Fifth, Fourth, Third, Second and First, and in the center of First Street at one-half the distance between the railroad tracks and the building. They were also placed at Columbus and Central, New Orleans and Third, Orleans at First, Olive and Congress, and Fourth.

At the turn of the twentieth century, the country was in the mood to celebrate. St. Louis, the fourth-largest city in the U.S., began plans to host the Louisiana Purchase Exposition or 1904 St. Louis World's Fair. Some 10,000 builders would create a fantastic city on 1,272 acres of what is now Forest Park and the Washington University campus. The largest and most beautiful fair to date, it contained 1,576 buildings connected by seventy-five miles of roads and walkways.

From opening day on April 30 until the fair closed on December 1, an average of 85,000 visitors a day paid the fifty cents admission for the right to be transported between exhibits by automobile, camel, electric automobile, electric launch, elephant, gondola, railroad, turtle, and wheelchair.

Carnival amusements could be found on the mile-long Pike. A fairgoer could ride the world's largest Ferris wheel (2,160-person capacity), visit the Tyrolean Alps village, or tour parts of France, Jerusalem, the Philippines, and Japan. They could experience the great Galveston Flood, meet the legendary Geronimo, and see epic naval battles and Abraham Lincoln's actual cabin.

The offices of the *Pacific Transcript* in 1891, where the city's weekly newspaper was published. The paper continued to be published until 1985, although not in this building. *From the MVG&HS collection.*

The three-story McHugh-Dailey Mercantile Emporium was built in 1907 using materials salvaged from the 1904 St. Louis World's Fair. The second floor provided living quarters for the McHugh and Dailey families. The clear-span, 8,000-square-foot third-floor opera house hosted town government meetings, high school graduations, and entertainment for decades. The third floor was closed in 1980 due to fire safety concerns, but reopened in 2009 when an elevator was installed. *From the MVG&HS collection.*

It was said to be the only world's fair that made a profit. When it was all over, fair organizers began the process of dismantling the buildings, selling some materials as salvage. Two savvy East Franklin County merchants, who had decided to build a commodious structure in Pacific for their growing retail empire, made their way to the crumbling fairgrounds.

Lawrence P. McHugh and James J. Dailey selected enough building materials to fill eleven rail cars for delivery to Pacific. The three-story mercantile emporium, residence, and opera house that they built opened for business in 1910, a banner year for new businesses in Pacific.

E. B. LeSaulnier built his residence and drugstore on St. Louis Street. J. W. Glaser Sand Mines, Missouri Silica Company, and Universal Sand Company began mining silica sand. Robert Schuchardt opened his ice company. John A. Thiebes opened his furniture store at First and Union streets. Gus Rau opened his soda water bottling company. Along First and St. Louis streets that year, groceries, meat markets, jewelers, tailors, and notion stores opened. Herman Langenbacher opened a restaurant. The Rexon sisters opened a hotel.

At the turn of the new century, Pacific residents were accustomed to rapid change and progress. They could deposit their savings in one of three banks: Pacific Bank, founded in 1892; Citizens Bank, founded in 1909; or Farmers & Merchants, founded in 1914. If they didn't fancy working for the railroad, steady work could be found at the soda water works or the canning factory.

In the City of Pacific, where every family had at least one relative who worked for one of the city's two railroads, an era of unprecedented promise was approaching. During the period between the turn of the century and World War I, when the railroads were temporarily nationalized, grandeur rode the rails.

These were the years that the great name trains attained their glamour. The steam locomotive was in its prime and was king—whether they were new stars of the silent screen, a family on the way to visit grandma, or a carload of coal, America was on the move, the trains were moving it, and the steam engine was pulling it. It has been dubbed the Golden Age of Railroading.

Pacific was racing into the twentieth century. The Pacific Home Telephone Company began offering service in 1905.

In May 1911, the Frisco Railroad was asked to furnish the city with water. Bonds were issued on November 9, 1911, in the amount of $15,000 for a water works plant. An oil engine was purchased from the Remington Oil Engine Company for $1,251, and fire hydrants from the Iowa Fire Hydrant Company.

The new water works soon would be tested. On Saturday evening on August 15, 1911, fire was discovered in a coal shed at the rear of the Red Front Saloon on St. Louis Street. At first it was thought to be a small matter but in spite of all that could be done it spread to the adjoining buildings. For a while it was thought that the entire block, which contained some of the most desirable establishments in the city, would go up in flames.

Every adult man, white and black, showed up to fight the fire and still the water and hoses of the Missouri Pacific Railroad and the Frisco Railroad fire crew were needed.

The Missouri Hardstone Brick Company was built in 1930. For about three decades, using a combination of gravity, German machinery, and heat, the plant made very hard white bricks using the pure silica sand from the Pacific outcrop. The building was demolished in 2007 to make way for a business center. *From the MVG&HS collection.*

All the exterior buildings of L. P. Gross' Commercial Hotel at St. Louis and Columbus streets were destroyed and Gross lost about $500 in stock at his bakery next door. The Brennan brothers, who had operated the Red Front Saloon since 1890, suffered the greatest loss, their building and fixtures amounting to $1,000.

In 1910, Fred Mayle opened a grocery store on South First Street, almost in front of the stately brick railroad station. His son Clarence, who did not fancy himself a grocer, painted the picture of a car on the side of the grocery store and began selling automobiles. At first it was a romantic business of big touring cars and gearless jitneys, but the practical railroad men and farmers who bought cars chose the $400 Fords. Within a decade, Mayle was a dedicated Ford dealer. He bought a building at First and Union that included a commodious house in the rear. He would later move the house to Osage Street to make way for a new building for his dealership. The house is still occupied.

An auto ownership report in 1916 indicated that there were twenty auto owners in Pacific. Of those, thirteen owned Fords. Two auto owners were driving Hupmobiles, leaving one owner each for Chevrolet, United, Studebaker, Buick, and Locomobile.

Railroad expansion reached its highest point in 1916 with 245,000 miles of track in the U.S. and then began the slow decline. Passenger and freight mileage saw a slight surge during World War I but mismanagement of the roads prompted President Woodrow Wilson to temporarily nationalize the railroads.

The downtown commuter lot is the site of the old turntable that the two railroads used to turn engines around for return trips, or to back them into the roundhouse stalls for repairs.

Patriotism surged during World War I as ladies folded bandages for the Red Cross, the men held war bond rallies, and the boys volunteered for service. The *Pacific Transcript* printed the letters from men in service.

With the war over and a new administration in Washington, the railroad owners thought they could offset the decline in freight and passenger revenue by cutting the wages of the workers. They chose the shop repair men as the weakest of the unions. On June 1, 1922, they cut the shopmen's wages by seven cents an hour and 400,000 employees walked off the job.

"The Pacific boys walked off the job this morning," the *Pacific Transcript* reported in a two-inch item on its front page. As the strike dragged on through-out the summer, the shopmen attended their gardens and went fishing, seemingly unaware of the fate that awaited them.

In the end, Pacific was singled out for a stunning retribution. The Missouri Pacific closed its repair shops in Pacific, moving the equipment and the jobs to St. Louis, Sedalia, and De Soto.

It was an event that would be remembered as economically devastating, and worse for the city than the Great Depression that was looming. Thereafter, Pacific became just a water and passenger stop for both Missouri Pacific and the Frisco. But the town still had the river and the silica deposit, so men tried to find work in the gravel plants and silica mines.

Silica SAND

*W*hen the Phoenician sailors in 5,000 B.C. placed their cooking pots on blocks of soda ash and accidentally turned the sand into molten glass, they created an industry that would fill the world with colorful beads, bottles, food utensils, art glass, and mirrors. In every era, man continued finding uses for glass that would eventually lead to crystal churches, glass-skinned skyscrapers, and computers in every household.

Sand is the major component of glass, making up 60 to 75 percent of the finished product after melting. The absence of color creates the transparence, brilliancy, and hardness of glass. The best glass is made from the softest, whitest sand or sweet sand, like that found at Pacific.

The Pacific bluffs are pure white St. Peter sandstone. The deposit, which rises boldly above ground in a quarter-mile-wide outcrop at Pacific, continues in a crescent-shaped belt that is fifteen miles wide at places and stretches from Warren County to Cape Girardeau, edging against the Mississippi River at Crystal City, whose name reflects its origin in mining sand for glass. The deposit covers about six square miles in Franklin County.

The outcrop at Pacific is remarkably pure quartz sand. Farther south, on Highway O, a reddish stain in the white bluff face indicates the presence of iron in the sand, but at Pacific the sand is 99.96 percent pure.

Beginning in the 1860s, in both tunnel and open pits, the sandstone was blasted down from the face, loaded into the quarry cars by hand, and hauled to a plant by drum and cable. In some plants, the rock was crushed in a jaw crusher, dried in a rotary oil-burning dryer, passed through a fourteen-mesh screen, and elevated to bins, from which chutes carried it to rail

A 1918 Missouri Geology and Mines Bureau report identified the abandoned silica caves, above, as being part of the Pacific Glass Sand Company.

U.S. Silica, which currently mines silica sand at Pacific.

A handcart at the entrance to an early Pacific silica mine. *From the MVG&HS collection.*

cars sitting on a spur of the Missouri Pacific Railroad. But much of the sand at Pacific was so white and friable that no crushing was necessary.

Glass sand mines were operated at Pacific as early as the 1860s and 1870s. Early mining created the tunnels behind the present-day Beacon Car Wash and NAPA Truck Repair building. Glass sand plants at Pacific in the early decades of the last century were Gray Summit White Sand Company, J. W. Glaser, Tavern Rock Sand Company, and Pacific Glass Sand Company. At that time sand was used in steel foundries, marble cutting and grinding, the white finish on terra cotta, and glass manufacturing.

In 1898, the Pittsburgh Plate Glass Company developed a process for producing thinner glass with the plate process expanding the use of glass in architecture. Over the first decades of the past century, sand mining at Pacific flourished. Among the mining companies were Fred Schendler, Stuhlmann and Ahrens, C. H. Wilson, Pacific White Sand Company, St. Louis Glass Sand, J. W. Glaser, J. R. Young, Macks Creek Sand and Clay, Denton Sand and Gravel, and W. W. Goran Sand and Gravel.

U.S. Silica periodically hosts a Chamber of Commerce luncheon to allow businessmen and businesswomen to witness a blast knocking the sandstone down from the bluff face.

Today, U.S. Silica operates a large plant at Pacific and ships sand that finds its way into catalytic converters in Japan, castings for fine gun barrels in Germany, silicon globes for computers, and plate glass.

"The bulk of what we mine at Pacific is still used for glass," said Chris Rahn, U.S. Silica's general manager. "Most of it is used in the U.S. but we do ship all over the world."

Red tractor-trailers driving through Pacific carry twenty-seven loads of silica sand a day to a glass manufacturer in Kansas City. Four train hopper cars a day take sand to another plant in Shreveport, Louisiana, while an additional four or five train cars head for Park Hills, Missouri.

"We ship half a million tons a year from this plant," Rahn said. "Every Kohler sink or bathtub that you see has Pacific silica sand in its china skin."

Rahn says the Pacific outcrop still contains enough silica sand to continue mining at the current level for another one hundred years.

Route 66

The first U.S. auto owners who struck out on the open road did so at their own risk. By 1917, only 2 percent of the nation's roads were paved. Courageous motorists looked at maps with lines drawn between Baltimore, Maryland, and California along what was known as the Old Trails Road. There was no correlation among Old Trail maps of the various states, leaving motorists often lost and disgusted.

Thanks to Cyrus Avery, an Oklahoma businessman, a push was made to connect Chicago and Southern California through his state of Oklahoma; a distance of 2,400 miles. The new road was designated U.S. Highway 66.

It would pass through Missouri and Pacific, following much of John C. Fremont's old trails. When construction of the road reached Pacific, bypassing Manchester Road, a portion of what was known as Prospect Hill was carved and blasted away to create a roadbed that slipped between the city on the south and the silica bluff on the north—creating the city landmark known locally as Sand Mountain.

As autos began to pass by on the new road, one local family saw opportunity. In 1934, James and Bill Smith cut logs on the family farm and trucked them to a site on the new road, immediately east of Pacific. In 1935, they added a bar room and advertised heavily that the inn was the only place along the route for miles to get a mixed drink. The Red Cedar Inn closed in 1972 when James Smith II retired. James Smith III and his sister Ginger reopened it in 1987, but it closed again in 2005.

In 2003, the Red Cedar Inn was placed on the National Register of Historic Places. As Kathy Weiser wrote,

> Towering sandstone bluffs line Route 66 through Pacific, dotted with caves, making many a Mother Road traveler do a double take. The caves are from Pacific's silica mining days, dating back to the 1870s. They were exposed in 1932 when Route 66 was realigned through Pacific, bypassing the Manchester Road alignment.

Route 66 above, as seen looking east from Blackburn Park.

St. Louis horticulturist Henry Shaw purchased several historic farms west of Pacific as a haven for his orchid plants in danger from the air pollution near his St. Louis Shaw's Garden. He hired Lars Peter Jensen, who had emigrated to the U.S. to landscape homes for St. Louis brewer Adolphus Busch. Jensen conceived a plan to beautify the roadway between Shaw's Garden in St. Louis and the Arboretum west of Pacific.

The Civilian Conservation Corps (CCC) was assigned to build a stone lookout tower on the bluff above Route 66. The lookout would be named Jensen's Point in honor of Jensen. Completion of the lookout was cause for a grand celebration, in which autos containing dignitaries and parades from neighboring communities lined Route 66 for a mile in each direction.

In 1945, members of Queen's Daughters, a St. Bridget Catholic Church sodality, looked at the caves in the bluff face and had an inspiration. The soft sandstone cave was reminiscent of the deserts of the Holy Land. "Wouldn't it be grand," they said, "to have a life-sized nativity scene in the cave opening?" What started out as a religious project captivated the heart of the town. A citywide fundraising campaign was begun to help the ladies buy the statues.

The Civilian Conservation Corps (CCC) built the lookout atop the bluff as part of the Shaw Ozark Gateway. It was named Jensen's Point in honor of horticulturist Lars Peter Jensen. *From the MVG&HS collection.*

The Red Cedar Inn opened shortly after the new highway was completed. In 2003, the inn was placed on the National Register of Historic Places. *From the MVG&HS collection.*

When the younger men climbed up narrow ladders carrying the statues to be placed in the cave, word seemed to spread spontaneously, and soon cars from St. Louis were driving our Route 66 to see the nativity scene in the bluff.

Over the years, the Chamber of Commerce and the City of Pacific accepted responsibility for the statues. Today, a group of businessmen house and place the statues, using high-lift equipment.

Route 66 through Pacific is now the I-44 Business Bypass, but tourism is being rejuvenated as visitors from across the U.S. and from abroad travel Historic Route 66. Pacific businesses and civic groups often play host to the Route 66 Association of Missouri as it plans trips for motorists and club members.

A 1930s postcard depicts Sand Mountain. *From the MVG&HS collection.*

The Queen's Daughters originated the nativity scene on the bluff in 1945, creating the city's first tourist attraction. The practice continues to this day.

Interstate 44

As Interstate 44 passes through a cut in the silica escarpment just inside the Franklin County line, the City of Pacific comes into view.

The alignment gives Pacific maximum visibility, which is a great asset in economic development, according to Sheila Steelman, Pacific community and economic development director, and plays a great role in the city's economic future.

"When retailers learn that you're located on an interstate highway, the first thing they want to know about are properties with highway visibility," Steelman said. "Pacific is blessed to have several properties along the city's western edge parallel with I-44."

The highway stretches across the south central part of Missouri and is a major corridor traveling from the Midwest to the West Coast—as were the Pacific Railroad and Historic Route 66 that preceded it.

Between 1949 and 1956, the Federal Highway Administration constructed five interstate highways to bypass U.S. Route 66. One of those was Interstate 44 (I-44).

Currently construction is underway that will transform the entrance to the city, opening access to vacant commercial sites and creating a retail tourism district along Historic Route 66, which parallels I-44 for more than one mile at the Pacific interchange.

Some 65,000 vehicles pass Pacific on I-44 each day.

In a partnership with the City of Pacific, the Missouri Department of Transportation (MoDOT) is currently completing four separate but related road improvement projects that will transform the entrance to Pacific and enhance economic development.

Eastbound exit and entrance ramps are being completely rebuilt, placing the interchange directly east of City Hall. Design of the new ramps eliminates a dangerous curve at the old exit and a short acceleration lane at the old entrance. Additional lanes will be added to I-44 extending to Union, Missouri.

Interstate 44 runs through Pacific, parallel with Historic Route 66. The Missouri Department of Transportation is currently rebuilding the eastbound entrance and exit ramps as well as West Osage Street (Route 66) where it parallels the interstate.

West Osage Street, which is also U.S. 66 and U.S. 50, will be widened to five lanes, with left turn lanes at Viaduct Street. This stretch of roadway will also be transformed. Using stimulus funds, a new road will be built with new lanes added, and new curbs and sidewalks will be included on both sides of the roadway from Seventh Street to Indian Warpath Drive. This will create a commercial district that combines existing banks, restaurants, and the West Osage Center with new developments on land that has been vacant for decades. Creating a pedestrian-friendly architectural theme, some sixty trees will be planted and ninety new streetlights installed.

The third project is construction of a pedestrian walkway on Thornton Road and Viaduct Street, which will allow residents and guests at the hotel on the north side of I-44 to walk to the restaurants and retail area on the south side. The city is paying for half of the ramp and pedestrian walk project, using taxes generated by a Commercial Improvement District (CID).

I-44 and Historic Route 66 run side by side in this photo taken at Payne Street. The interstate was constructed to upgrade the former highway of song.

The fourth road project is the widening of I-44 to six lanes from Pacific to the I-50 exit leading to the City of Union at the Bourbeuse River.

The City Tourism Committee recently received approval from MoDOT to locate an electronic billboard next to the new exit ramp that will advertise city events and invite motorists to visit Old Town. Tourism tax funds, approved by voters in 2008, will be used to pay for the billboard.

The combination of city, MoDOT, stimulus funds, and city tourism projects tie I-44 and Historic Route 66 together in a larger-than-life building program that the city could never have done on its own, according to Mayor Herbert Adams.

"This is a great time for our city," Adams said. "It's long-held dreams realized."

OLD *Town* RENEWAL

$\mathcal{I}$n the early decades of the last century, Christmas shoppers on St. Louis Street could find almost anything they desired. If there was snow, Joe Dailey would allow the boys to tie their sleds to the back bumper of his Model A Ford, drive down St. Louis Street, swing around the little First Street monument, and drive back to Sixth Street.

In honor of the season, a group of merchants placed a Christmas tree atop the small stone structure. One December morning townspeople awoke to find the Christmas tree gone. Within a few minutes someone glanced up and saw it perched at the edge of the bluff on what is today Blackburn Park.

By the time the holiday season was over, the idea had caught hold. The year after that a group of men cut a tree and hauled it up to the top of the bluff. The following year they needed a larger tree and persuaded a property owner in Little Ireland to allow them to trek through his woods and find a large tree.

In recent decades, the live tree was abandoned and the Lions Club installed a tall pole with a collar carrier that raised a series of strings of lights. The first Saturday in December, the Lions climb to the top of the bluff to raise the Christmas tree of lights. There on the bluff top the workers shudder against the cold and allow themselves a glimpse at the town below.

Blackburn Park, atop the bluff, offers a unique view of Old Town Pacific. In little more than a dozen city blocks, historic buildings, railroad tracks, and the commuter parking lot, which once held the railroad turntable and roundhouse, can be seen.

Here Inks and Blumenthal laid out a small city in square blocks within walking distance of the new Pacific Railroad depot. Progress of the young railroad was hampered by the Civil War when railroad property was destroyed, but the railroad quickly rebuilt its Pacific properties, and in 1870 constructed a fine brick depot, or Union Station, to serve both railroads. In 1977, the depot was dismantled and removed.

Today, Old Town Pacific is experiencing a renaissance. Most of the present-day buildings were constructed between 1880 and 1922 during the Golden Age of Railroading when the Missouri Pacific repair shops and bridge works were located in Pacific. Three hotels were among the buildings that have since been torn down. The merchants who built these buildings frequently occupied the second floors of their buildings. Others rented rooms or apartments to railroad employees. Some buildings touched each other or were so close that craftsmen had to lay up bricks from inside the buildings. In the past ten years, a new wave of businesspeople has renovated the historic buildings, returning them to an active life in the business community.

David McHugh, great-grandson of Lawrence P. McHugh, owns and operates The Great Pacific Coffee Company on the first floor of the McHugh-Dailey Building. Offices occupy the second floor. The third-floor opera house is under renovation. An elevator has been added, which will enable the third floor to return to its original use as a public entertainment site.

Streets are busy in downtown Pacific during community events, as seen in this view of Old Town taken from Blackburn Park during Cruise Night 2007.

The influence of the founding merchants is still present in downtown Pacific. William Mauthe built this brick house in the nineteenth century. Today, it is being restored and used as a residence.

Lorenz Leber and Henry Hirth constructed the Royal Theater in 1929 in the crowning decade of the motion picture business they launched in 1913. The theater closed in the 1960s. Today, the building houses a flooring company.

115 and 117 East St. Louis Street were two of several buildings restored by Keith Muehler. The Muehler Insurance Agency is located at 117 East St. Louis Street.

John Heger has restored the 113 West St. Louis Street former retail store and residence.

At 301 West St. Louis, Brengard Tile and Flooring occupies the former movie theater. Lorenz Leber and Henry Hirth had started showing moving pictures in Pacific in 1913, first in a tent, then in a frame building. They purchased the bricks from the demolished Missouri Pacific Machine Shop building in 1929 and built a commodious structure to house their growing moving picture business. They named it the Royal Theater. Immediately after the building opened, the owners installed sound equipment to support the new talkies. After closing as a movie theater and housing several short-lived theatrical groups, the building sat empty until Brengard bought it, restored the exterior, and restructured the interior for his flooring business.

Keith Muehler, whose business occupies 117 East St. Louis Street, has restored several buildings. The earliest known owner of his office building was Ted Roemer, a barber, who had his shop in front and lived in the rest of the building. Jack Nowling also operated a barbershop in the building, which Muehler bought in 1993. American Steel Pipe Supply now occupies the second-floor office. Muehler also owns 115 East St. Louis Street next door, which he bought in 1998 and restored. Gene Schneider Shoe occupied this building in the 1950s.

John Heger Realtors now occupies 113 West St. Louis Street. This building was built in 1904, with two storefronts on the first level and two apartments on the second floor. The building served as Leach's (later Leah's) Clothing Store, Waters Barbershop, Anderson's Drug Store, and others. Heger bought this building in 1999 and has restored both the interior and exterior. Apartments still occupy the second floor.

Noonan Appraisers occupies 115 West St. Louis Street. This one-story building was probably built as a U.S. post office, which occupied it for several decades. The Noonan family bought the building in the 1950s–1960s and restored the interior for offices, "but the exterior was so sound that very little had to be done to it," Tom Noonan said. It was the Shaffer Real Estate office in the 1970s.

Ron and Charlene Sansone have lived in the 137 West St. Louis Street building since 1971. LeSaulnier constructed the two-story building as a residence and the attached one-story structure

Ron and Charlene Sansone have restored the former LeSaulnier residence and pharmacy and Iron Gate Antiques, one of the oldest extant buildings in the city.

as his pharmacy. The Sansones completely renovated the building, maintaining the exterior balcony and shutters. They also own the one-story structure with an iron gate immediately east of their home, which is believed to be one of the oldest buildings in the city and once served as a stagecoach stop. The Sansones operated the

Officials gather beneath the vintage clock at First and St. Louis streets for the dedication of new St. Louis Street improvements.

The historic Clarence Mayle Home has been continuously maintained and occupied.

The historic former Adolphe Westmeyer home has been restored to its original beauty.

David McHugh, great-grandson of Lawrence McHugh, greets customers in The Great Pacific Coffee Company, which occupies the first floor of the McHugh-Dailey Building.

Strawberry Patch gifts, art, and craft supply shop and the Iron Gate Antiques Shop from 1970 to 1981 in the two adjoining buildings.

Brad Reed Insurance at 102 West St. Louis Street is a one-story building with a new exterior constructed over a historic sandwich shop and saloon that served as a gas station in the 1930s as automobiles became more prevalent in Pacific. Steve and Pat Reed rehabilitated the building for their American Family Insurance Company. Today, their son operates Brad Reed Insurance in the building.

The 110 West St. Louis Street building now houses the offices of Bingaman Contracting. Joe Ottman, a well-known carpenter and builder, constructed the two-story section of the building as his family residence. The adjoining one-story structure housed his extensive woodworks, which had a power drive that ran down the center of the building and provided power for a series of saws and wood lathes. Sunny Oberkramer completely renovated this building.

At 112 West St. Louis Street, Cindy Klink operates her Klink Music Studio on the ground floor with the second floor serving as her residence. The building was originally built as a residence. The Oswald family lived there for years. During a renovation, the open porches were closed in, protecting a beautiful pine staircase. The signatures of Oswald's son-in-law Jerry Miller and Bud Strauman were

New duplexes occupy the lot that formerly housed crumbling trailers and a home ravaged by floodwater.

revealed on the plaster when Keith Muehler bought and renovated the building in 2002. "It's a testament to the craftsmen who built these buildings that they are still as square as the day they were built even though they have been shaken by trains for more than one hundred years," Muehler said.

New construction is also breathing renewed life into Old Town as local builders begin to construct new single-family homes and duplexes in the neighborhoods for the first time in half a century. The neat frame structures are elevated above the one-hundred-year flood plain to protect them from future high water.

Gullet Construction and builders Jeff Snyder and Jimmy Smith offer a simple design of affordable homes that fit the surroundings. Sandwiched between existing buildings, upwards of twenty new single-family homes have taken shape, replacing aging trailers and dilapidated outbuildings.

Older residences, like the business buildings, are also undergoing renovation. On First Street, three historic residences have recently been restored to their original appearance and are occupied as residences. Another former residence has been restored and converted to a doctor's office. The historic Clarence Mayle house has been maintained and appears as it did when it was built.

LEFT: Flanked by Mayor Herb Adams and City Administrator Harold Selby, State Senator John Griesheimer tours construction of a new single-family home on Pacific's south side.

BELOW: Two pairs of brothers—Jim and Bill McHugh and Tom and Mike Dailey—continue to restore the 1907 McHugh-Dailey Building constructed by their grandfathers. The restoration is designed to serve as a catalyst for renewed economic and cultural life in Old Town.

A GOOD *Place* TO LIVE

$\mathcal{I}$n the 1960s, Pacific began to change as a place to live. Many of the fine old homes in Old Town had been demolished. Adelaide Street, or Silk Stocking Row as it was known in the nineteenth century, had been turned into Columbus and had become a business district.

Pacific began to take on a new shape when insurance company owner Garland "Ick" Noonan created the first modern subdivision. Noonan had purchased the city's flagship insurance agency, the Close Insurance Company, founded by C. C. Close in 1870. Hawthorne Subdivision, on Congress Street, turned a former cornfield into a residential neighborhood.

In the 1990s, developers from the St. Louis area discovered the open spaces adjacent to Pacific and designed a series of upscale subdivisions.

Lawless Homes, headquartered in Valley Park, brought the city's first one-hundred-plus-home subdivision when they built Silver Lake Estates Subdivision. Built on a series of gently rolling hills, the development includes a small lake and clubhouse. An active homeowners' association and Neighborhood Watch organization brings residents into community affairs. Here, too, residents joined together to promote safe driving on their streets and child safety.

On the former Smith farm on South Highway N, Mayer Homes built The Villages at West Lake, a 257-home development that includes a swimming pool and clubhouse.

Officer Cynthia Garner fingerprints children as members of the Silver Lakes Subdivision Neighborhood Watch hold a child safety and barbecue fundraiser to benefit the Sgt. Dan Donnelly Backpack Fund.

When the developers offered special deals for victims of the March 2008 flood, Pacific florist Ken Coleman decided to leave the area where he had grown up and move into a large house in a new subdivision. Coleman had turned the small frame house he inherited from an aunt into a show place, adding brick siding, brass lamps, and wrought iron fence rails, but he accepted the FEMA buyout and moved to West Lake.

On Highway OO, Osage Hills was built on a crest line of a wooded area. Residents enjoyed a sense of living in the country while still living in the city. Immediately north, Barklage Development created the Forest Glen Subdivision, carving home sites on a series of ruggedly wooded ridge lines.

In even steeper territory, McBride & Sons developed Eagles View Subdivision, an appropriately named development of single-family homes and attached villas perched on a hilltop high above the entrance to the city on the westbound I-44 interchange.

Smaller subdivisions along Old Gray Summit Road offered beautiful home sites. In 2002, Indian Hills Subdivision, a large lot development on the former Charles Close farm, was annexed into the city.

Volunteers barbecue to benefit the school backpack program.

Millstone Village Senior Apartments is an example of the variety of housing available in Pacific.

The Villages at West Lake is one of a half-dozen one-hundred-plus-home subdivisions under construction in Pacific.

CITY *Park* SYSTEM

$\mathcal{E}$very good-weather morning in Pacific Community Park finds walkers making their way around the half-mile paved walking trail. Some will stay long enough to make the circle six times to achieve the three miles said to ensure good health and aid in weight loss. What they see as they walk is the city coming to life.

Members of the Pacific Garden Club might be tending the flowers that they planted in the entrance divider box. Small children might be on the merry-go-round, one of the most popular spots in the park.

From Memorial Day to Labor Day, swimmers and divers can be seen in the city swimming pool near the park entrance. On early mornings during the season, this is where the Pacific Swim Club practices, and on summer evenings, the club hosts its home meets against swimmers in the West County League.

At the center of the circle—where Harry Birk formerly planted a cornfield—youngsters play baseball and the St. Bridget Soccer Association plays its home games. In this circle the Moving Wall, the traveling replica of the National Vietnam Veterans Memorial, attracted thousands of visitors in a three-day visit between October 17 and 19, 2006. Young Pacific High JROTC cadets stood as honor guards in four-hour shifts around the clock. On the final day, Mayor Herbert Adams presided over a grand presentation that honored all veterans and the organizers of the Moving Wall. The Pacific High School Band, in full uniform, played music. The park circle was filled with well-wishers.

Entrance to the city park on Congress Street.

A new children's merry-go-round was delivered in 2008. Park Board members provide the first push.

Walkers make their way to the fireworks exhibit.

The Pacific Park System has a history as old as the City of Pacific. On an 1883 map, a small square at the southeast corner of Union and Second streets is marked City Park. In the center of the park is a small circle, signifying some long-erased shrub or monument. One element of what is arguably the city's first park remains. After World War II, the American Legion Post 320 Auxiliary began a program to erect an honor roll of those who left from Pacific to serve in World War I and World War II. The city fathers assigned the northwest corner of the little park for the monument. It still stands there today, the result of a 2007 renovation that replaced a menu marquee monument with carved granite. The monument faces a small circular garden.

Blackburn Park, at the top of Sand Mountain, is a five-acre mesa at the top of what was formerly known as Prospect Hill. In 1934, when the front of the sand-stone escarpment was blown away to make way for Route 66, the bluff face that identifies the city was exposed. In early diaries and newspaper stories, the hill was known as Prospect Hill. The name was apt, since the hilltop offered a spectacular prospect of the Meramec Valley to the east, south, and west.

The city park on West Congress Street is the site of the city swimming pool, three pavilions, a children's play area, tennis courts, and ball fields.

In the mid-1960s, the city purchased the former Harry Birk home and farm property. The circle that bears his name was

The city swimming pool, located in the city park, is open from Memorial Day to Labor Day and is one of the city's most popular family attractions.

Mary Miller's garden, in full bloom each spring, greets park visitors at the northwest corner of the city park.

Boy Scouts salute the flag at a rededication of the downtown Soldiers' Memorial.

once a cornfield. The home sat where the swimming pool is located. Birk kept a small herd of dairy cattle and grew his own feed. Relatives of the Birk family still live near the park and enjoy the permanent green space on what was once the family farm.

Later, the city would purchase farmland from the Ed Miller family at the west end of the park. Jean Ann Link and her parents, John and Dorothy Miller, lived on the farm that is now the west end of the park, where the Rulon Pavilion is located.

Some days, Link brings her granddaughter Morgan, two, who prefers the swings that occupy her great-great-grandfather's old former cow pasture.

"It's a great place to be," Jean Link said.

For an entire winter, the late Lloyd Duncan, a local contractor, donated equipment and a crew to demolish the buildings, clear away the debris, and grade the park. City Public Works Commissioner Ed Gass borrowed a disc, harrow, and seeder and finish-graded the ball fields and seeded them.

In 1999, Boys Town of Missouri donated an additional twelve acres to the park located on the south side of Brush Creek. This park area is only partially developed. The St. Bridget Soccer Association practiced here until they were allowed to move to the center circle. An annual fishing derby is held in the small pond on this area of the park.

As the home pool of the Pacific Swim Club, the city pool hosts swimming meets when the club competes in home meets.

The large pavilion at the west end of the park is the Rulon Pavilion, named for a former alderman. The small gazebo at the right of the entrance, which was donated by the Noonan family, has been named the LaVerne Wiest Pavilion, honoring her as a longtime Park Board and Pacific Garden Club member.

Pacific Station Plaza is a mini-park being developed on South First Street by the Pacific Partnership.

The ball fields are named for Pacific athletes Art Lewis, Bob Klinger, Linda Wells, and George Hinkle Jr.

Roadside Park at the foot of Sand Mountain was cleared as a picnic and rest area.

In 1999, the city acquired thirty-one acres off Meramec Street east of First Street and developed Liberty Field as a soccer field and equestrian center. Allowing the Pacific Soccer Association to move to the new fields opened the Birk Circle for the St. Bridget Soccer Association to play at-home games for the first time in thirty years.

The city owns additional donated parkland in the eastern section of the city that is yet undeveloped.

On South First Street, the Pacific Partnership is developing Pacific Station Plaza as a mini-park, train-watching venue. The Partnership annually holds a Railroad Day celebration in this park and has held a successful chainsaw carving competition and a Kansas City-sanctioned barbecue cook-off here. The site houses the donated Burlington Northern caboose, which was the last caboose ever built for the railroad.

The St. Bridget Soccer League plays an at-home game in the city park.

Young anglers participate in an annual fishing derby.

The American Legion Auxiliary rededicates the restored honor roll as the Soldiers' Memorial in the city's first park.

Jobs

$\mathcal{A}$s the population outgrew the row houses and historic homes in Old Town, developers began to build subdivisions along Brush Creek, on the neighboring ridge lines, and on former farm land, and some savvy civic leaders began to focus on bringing jobs to Pacific.

Joe Dailey, son of the former merchant still operating the family's three-story building, developed Dailey Industrial Park and lured a box factory to provide jobs in Pacific.

Forward-thinking Mayor Bill Wiest, an auto dealer, led the city in the development of the Integram Industrial Park. He went to Canada to bring Integram St. Louis Seating to Pacific. The firm would be the city's largest employer until it closed in 2008, a casualty of the U.S. auto manufacturers' meltdown.

With a plan crafted by Jo Ann Hoehne, former municipal clerk, and Ed Gass, former public works director, the city entered into an agreement with Boys Town of Missouri to develop land the organization had inherited. The Boys Town property became the Midwest Industrial Park.

Graphic Packaging.

Today, workers in the manufacturing plants in Pacific's four industrial parks build an array of products so varied that the list sounds like a brochure for industrial diversity—industrial labels, labeling machines, racecar and flight simulators, industrial computers and barcode hardware, oil and water separators, gasoline nozzles, custom staircases, and carnival games.

The common denominator among the products on display in a November 2004 "Made in Pacific" Expo, staged by the City of Pacific and the Chamber of Commerce, was the use of computer technology;

Baker's Ice.

not just to track inventory, bill customers, and record revenue, but also to design equipment, and in many cases to be a component of the finished product.

Trekk Equipment manufactures a machine no bigger than a vacuum sweeper that stamps the labels in the necks of tee shirts and the waistbands of pants, replacing the old sewn-in cloth labels. The machines are manufactured in Pacific and shipped all over the U.S.

Bugeye Technology is creating new products faster than manufacturers can get them to market. Bugeye kept visitors busy driving its racecar simulator. The same technology creates F-15 flight simulators for the U.S. Naval Museum, and the company is currently developing personal vehicle simulators to retrain stroke victims at the University of Georgia Medical Center.

Red Bone Products distributes carnival games and components to build games.

Other industrial plants are Amteco, Inc., Baker's Ice, Clayton Corporation, Enterprise Label, Husky Corporation, INDUCOMP, Industrial Technologies, Kirkwood Stair, Lowell Manufacturing, Pro Roller, Pacific Valley Dairy, Graphic Packaging, and Wallis Companies.

Aurora Technologies.

The 2004 "Made in Pacific" Expo was so successful that the Chamber of Commerce made the decision to stage the event at Pacific High School, where it would double as a job fair for graduating seniors.

"Some graduates will look for jobs right out of high school," said Tim Baker, Chamber past president. "But it's our hope that even those who go on to college will know what might be available for them to come back to Pacific and work."

One of the city's largest employers is the Meramec Valley R-III School District, which is headquartered in Pacific.

School DAYS

*I*f the highways, railroads, and river are the arteries of the community, the school is the heart. In this era where the Parents as Teachers Program starts working with infants, and Pacific High graduates carry with their twelfth-grade diplomas as much as a full year of college credits, the school is the center of family life.

As a frontier community, the little frame schoolhouse was its polling place, a de facto city hall where the town board met, and the location of occasional pie suppers. Franklin residents inherited the large-family culture of the surrounding community and adapted it to the romance of the railroad.

Within months after the city plat was filed and lots were sold, citizens of the new community met at Watson's store and agreed to borrow money from the Franklin County school fund to construct a frame schoolhouse at the corner of (present-day) Fourth and Osage streets. Like the little railroad community it served, the first public school was a bustling, over-crowded schoolhouse that taught as many as ninety students at one time. As the community gained confidence in its newfound prosperity, the city fathers made the momentous decision to construct a brick school and they knew just the builder to construct it.

In 1870, H. W. Close was given a contract to build a brick schoolhouse with two rooms on the first floor and two rooms on the second floor at a cost of $5,999.79. Mr. Close was a bridge builder for the Wabash Railroad when the Missouri Pacific Railroad hired him to help construct bridges over the creeks and gorges where the railroad entered the Ozarks. He became a private contractor, built a series of buildings in the city including the original Pacific Presbyterian Church, and remained to make his home here.

He set the brick school well back on the lot, facing south toward the center of town, and leaving a wide front school yard. In 1905, Close was awarded a contract to construct a four-classroom addition at the back of the school. In 1920, a second addition was placed in front of the original building, bringing the schoolhouse up to the sidewalk. The builder placed the year, 1920, in the circle at the top of the front façade.

The old school still evokes its share of emotion as a place where milestones were passed and lifelong relationships forged. Most area residents of a certain age attended school in the building. Some attended all twelve years and graduated from high school there.

Some eighty years after the 1920 addition, retired U.S. Air Force Surgeon General Ken Pletcher, great-grandson of the school's builder, H. W. Close, recalled that he and a friend had scratched their initials in the damp concrete, causing a ruckus among the grownups.

"I don't think that it did any harm to the building," he chuckled.

In 1938, the west wing, gymnasium, two sets of restrooms, and two classrooms were added as a W.P.A. project. In a weeklong March 1939 celebration of that expansion, former graduates and a former superintendent held a series of reunions, "Gay Nineties" parties, and fried chicken dinners.

The first brick schoolhouse had four rooms. *From the MVG&HS collection.*

Prior to that, twelfth-grade students had graduated in the third-floor opera house in the McHugh-Dailey Building.

"I remember there was so much fuss about it we had to take off our shoes and walk onto the new wood floor in our stocking feet to accept our diplomas," Jessie Elliot Preiss later recalled.

The Meramec Valley R-III School District administration office is located in Pacific. The school district is one of the city's largest employers and more so than any other institution, progress of the school district has paralleled community growth and change.

In 1955, a new high school building was completed on West Osage (now the Meramec Valley Middle School). Later, a new middle school was built on what is now Indian Warpath Drive. It was named the Marple Agee building in honor of a popular school superintendent. The Pacific Public School continued to be the school for grades kindergarten through eighth grade until Zitzman Elementary opened.

The school would be enlarged four times to create the Community School that is still in use today.

In 1995, the old schoolhouse was renamed the Community School when Dr. Carrie Eidson created an accelerated alternative high school. Now the building houses the District's Special Education Department.

Today, the Meramec Valley R-III School District operates ten schools, including an early childhood center, five elementary schools, the original Pacific Public School, a middle school, an eighth-grade center, and Pacific High School. The district provides its own transportation and houses buses on the former Nike Missile base adjacent to Nike Elementary.

The district has had many firsts. It was the first district in the area to launch the Parents as Teachers Program introduced by U.S. Senator Kit Bond from Missouri. Parents as Teachers is an international early-childhood parent education

The 2009 Pacific High School graduates hurl their caps into the air at the conclusion of their graduation ceremony. *Photo by HR Imaging.*

and family support program that serves families throughout pregnancy until their child enters kindergarten, usually at age five. The program is designed to enhance child development and school achievement through parent education and is accessible to all families.

Since education begins at home and parents are their children's first and most influential teachers, supporting and educating parents is a logical strategy. The Parents as Teachers Program is one key way to ensure that children enter school ready to learn. Parents as Teachers has been offered to families in the Meramec Valley R-III School District for twenty-five years.

In elementary schools, where character education is valuable, an innovation program introduced the game of chess to second- and third-grade students at Robertsville Elementary School. Titled The First Move Chess Program, the game of chess encourages students to use patterns and logical deductive reasoning to solve problems. Offered during the school day as a supplement to the existing core curriculum, the focus is not on competition or tournament play, but rather in the thinking skills that are an inherent part of chess. Teachers see students pick up math concepts more quickly, demonstrate a better aptitude for reading comprehension, develop a new sense of focus, and display more courtesy towards others.

The Meramec Valley Middle School houses sixth- and seventh-grade students while Riverbend—the district's newest building—serves as an eighth-grade center and houses the alternative high school, a program that has increased the district's graduation rate.

A large turn-out attended the ribbon-cutting to open Riverbend School, the district's newest school, which houses the eighth grade and the alternative high school.

The Model U.N. Club offers the ultimate in government studies. *Photo by HR Imaging.*

LEFT: Members of the boys' team settle into a comfortable pace for a race. *Photo by Moe Deppe.*

BELOW: Angie Stanley, a freshman, seems to fly over the hurdles. *Photo by HR Imaging.*

A program that helps Meramec Valley R-III students reach higher education goals is the A+ college tuition program. Meramec Valley was also the first district in the area to qualify its high school graduates for two years of free college tuition under the A+ Program.

"The goal of the district is to prepare every graduate for some form of post-secondary school," Superintendent Randy George said.

A college prep program offers students the opportunity to earn college credits while still in high school.

Carrie Gross, a resident who had wanted to be a nurse, left an endowment to the high school, which pays tuition for students who enter a degree program to become nurses. The Health Occupations Program has expanded to prepare students for a wide array of careers in the medical field.

Under the direction of Paula Nolley and Ed Kappeler, the Pacific High School Drama and Music Department stages productions twice each school year that fill the 350-seat high school auditorium. Pacific High music and athletic programs help students develop skills in practice and competition and keep students in the spotlight.

The Marine Corps JROTC program not only trains young people for military careers; it also represents Pacific High School in community affairs, trooping the colors to open events and marching in parades.

Project Lead the Way is a multi-year engineering program that was created for students who like to use their minds to build projects with their hands. The students take introduction to engineering, principles of engineering, digital engineering, and civil engineering and architecture. These are some of the many classes at Pacific that can be taken for advanced college credit.

Members of the Health Occupations class pose for the yearbook. *Photo by Emily Mueller.*

High school music and athletic programs help students' skills in practice and competition and keeps students in the spotlight.

The DECA Club for business students, Beta Club, Bible Club, Tribe, Ecology Club, Speech Team, Student Council, Creative Arts Program (CAP), and Model U.N. are among the groups that also help students develop skills for life.

The Meramec Valley R-III School District carries on a close partnership with the local parochial school, St. Bridget of Kildare Elementary School. This school has a long life in the community.

In 1885, St. Bridget Catholic Church opened an elementary parochial school in Pacific. The Rev. John Hennes was pastor. The building committee

Counselor Kris Miller awards Ryan Bradshaw the Red & Black Scholarship and Music Scholarship from the University of Central Missouri during Seniors Awards Night.

moved a two-story residence building from a spot on South Fourth Street to Union Street to serve as the schoolhouse. The parish spent $400 to equip the school. The building would house the St. Bridget school for the next sixty-five years. The Franciscan Sisters from Manitowoc, Wisconsin, were the first teachers.

In 1950, a new school building was erected with four classrooms and a spacious auditorium. Kitchen equipment was installed and the practice of serving a hot lunch was begun. The old school building was completely remodeled and used as a convent and chapel for the teaching sisters of Notre Dame.

In 1962, four classrooms were added, and in 1978, two more classrooms and a new cafeteria were added to the south of the building, giving the parish a nine-room school, one for each grade.

In December 1982, due to heavy rains and flooding in lower parts of Pacific, the St. Bridget school gymnasium and cafeteria were transformed into the Red Cross shelter for about ten days.

In 1985, with an enrollment of 140 students, the parish celebrated the centennial of the school.

St. Bridget Catholic School and the Meramec Valley R-III School District have been forever linked. St. Bridget students are included in many school district programs and the school holds many of its pageants and performances in the Pacific High School auditorium.

St. Bridget Parish has offered elementary school since 1885. This building was erected in 1950.

Sarah Gamewell looks over the 2007–2008 yearbook. *Photo by Susan Benedict.*

A *Shared* FAITH

$\mathcal{T}$here is a recurring theme in the early faithful of Pacific: they attended church services in each other's homes before they had frame or stone buildings. And, once the congregations built structures, they shared their facilities with each other.

As early as 1844, area Catholics began attending Mass in an eighteen-by-twenty-four-foot log church on the bank of the Meramec River on a site overlooking present-day Pacific. Within eight years, Rev. Philip Grace determined that the church was too small. Patrick McBrearty deeded seven acres of land for a new church south of the original church. Construction was begun on a cornerstone but halted because of the Civil War.

It's hard to put a beginning on the churches. The bustling parish of St. Patrick of Armagh in Catawissa couldn't help but notice that attendance was dwindling at its mission church, Downpatrick, a log church located about two miles north of the rail center. Parishioners decided to build a stone church four blocks from the train depot.

A romantic bit of local lore accompanies the construction of this church, which was started just as the Civil War broke out. The story goes that stones had been assembled to build the church but the building was put on hold due to the war. Union soldiers sent to guard the Pacific Railroad bridges and other property took notice of the stones. They decided to use them to create a fort on the little embankment where the church was to be constructed.

When word spread through the town that the soldiers were moving the church stones, an intrepid parishioner, known locally as Grandma Kennedy, demanded to talk with the Union officer in charge. She chastised him for disrupting the future church and the officer—not named in the story—ordered the men to return the stones to the construction site.

In 1866, the new brick building was completed. The old church north of town remained standing until 1886, but the parishioners adopted the new church in town. Today, St. Bridget has a modern brick church, built in 1961 with the old bell from the previous church installed on the grounds.

Handwritten notes record a meeting of members of the Presbyterian Church of Pacific in July 1864, when the Rev. J. F. Fenton was named pastor. This congregation had been meeting in people's homes and wanted a church. In 1867, the congregation gave a contract to H. W. Close to construct a church at the corner of Fourth and St. Louis streets. The note-taker tells us that the church was to be built of stone and the cornerstone was laid on September 13, 1865. The stonework was done by James Divine.

But then the writer had second thoughts. Other reports said they acquired the stone church, which had been a Union Church.

"From 1864 to 1903, when a new minute book was opened, we have almost no information," the earlier historian wrote.

One early manifestation of this church was an active Ladies Aid. The ladies conducted bazaars, solicited for ministers' salaries, solicited for orphanages, arranged the ministers' entertainment, quilted, contributed to the mission board, bought Union Electric preferred stock, set up a committee to study a building addition, subscribed

The four oldest congregations in the city are the Presbyterians (above), Catholics (page 70, top), Baptists (page 70, bottom), and Methodists (page 71).

St. Bridget of Kildare Catholic Church.

Pacific Baptist Church.

money for moving expenses for a new minister in 1923, provided food for the Young Presbyterian Conference in Pacific, and provided little chairs for Sunday School.

They also contributed to church improvements in 1927 and contributed to the minister's pension fund and a new roof in 1929 and a new church floor in 1930. By 1933, they were helping with the janitor's salary and repairing the furnace. In 1926, the solid oak floor of the church was raised two feet and a basement with windows was built under the entire church. In 1951, a service building was connected on the south side. In 1955, the stone exterior was covered with brick veneer and a narthex was added to the front of the building, the sanctuary was redecorated, and stained-glass windows were installed. A new manse was erected at 115 North Fourth Street in 1959.

Pacific Presbyterian Church serves the community by providing meeting spaces for many organizations.

Dates are also unclear for Historic First Baptist Church of Pacific at 421 South First Street. The deed for the property is dated 1874 but the cornerstone on the building bears the date 1864. The original deed to the property indicates that King William Adams, a prominent African American patriarch of a large family, purchased land for the church. The church had a series of pastors under the support of King Adams, his son Jesse, and his grandson Udell.

After Udell Adams' death, the church closed temporarily, and the building served as a prayer chapel for area families. In 2004, Elder James L. Perkins, of Robertsville, became pastor of First Baptist. Under his guidance the old church entered a renaissance. Volunteers helped Rev. Perkins add a new roof, carpet, furnace, and doors. Church members allowed Rosalind Jordan to open Little Beginnings Day Care in the church cafeteria.

The old church suffered severe damage during the flood of March 2008. In the traditional spirit of sharing facilities, the daycare was moved to the United Methodist Church on West St. Louis Street while repairs were made to First Baptist.

In all probability, an earlier African American church existed for a time in the south side of the city. The outline of an A.M.E. Church for African American families appears on the 1892 maps but no information on the church has survived.

Pacific Baptist Church organized as a congregation in 1870, meeting in the Presbyterian Rock Church. The group purchased a lot at the corner of St. Louis and Sixth streets in 1871 to construct a building. The church was dedicated on December 2, 1883. In 1951, an educational building was constructed, and in 1962, a new sanctuary was dedicated next to the original building. The old church building was used as part of the church office. Pacific Baptist recently completed a new youth center on Old Gray Summit Road and has plans to build a church complex there.

In March 2001, Pacific Baptist filled its sanctuary with visitors from Washington and other surrounds who came to hear Kina Forman, a New York-based missionary with Jews for Jesus who visited Christian churches once a year on a two-week Easter tour. Using authentic Passover elements, a trained soprano voice, and an impressive knowledge of scripture, Forman sang and talked her way through each detail of the Jewish Passover, stopping—with some prompts from the Pacific Baptist congregation—to explain how she and other Jews for Jesus find Christ represented there.

Pacific United Methodist Church was organized in the 1880s when the Rev. Albert Jump and Rev. Halbeck preached here. The first Methodist building was constructed on St. Louis Street in 1886. For many years, the choirs of the Presbyterian and Methodist churches combined and served these churches on alternating Sundays. In 1960, Mr. and Mrs. James V. Hogan Sr. deeded three acres of ground in

Pacific United Methodist Church.

the Hogan Subdivision for a new church and parsonage. The first worship service was held in the new educational building on April 23, 1961. The new sanctuary was consecrated on January 26, 1969.

There followed a succession of new churches. The Pacific Assembly of God Church was organized in 1930. In 2008, the Assembly of God began construction on a youth activities center at 1995 Highway N.

The original date of the Pacific Temple Church of God in Christ at 113 Bellevue is uncertain. The congregation held services in a church building on Orleans Street that dates back to the 1880s. The church made the move to Bellevue in the 1950s. When the Rev. Abram Perkins and his wife, Alline, came to minister in the small church in 1987, the building was old and in great need of repair.

Jay Newman (center), flanked by his brothers John and Joe, shares a Passover ceremony with about fifty Gentile guests at The Great Pacific Coffee Company.

The small congregation accumulated $22,000 to renovate the church. John Moore, the assistant pastor, was helping to build a new church at Highway 141 and Clayton Road, which was replacing its pews. Pacific Temple bought enough pews to fill its new sanctuary. Today, the neatly paneled church, with its freshly stained pews, new piano, and organ is crisp and clean. Rev. John Moore is the pastor.

The Pacific church of Jehovah Witnesses, which first began as a congregation in Villa Ridge, moved to Pacific and built a church at 112 North Payne Street. In 1991, this was sold to the Church of Christ congregation, and the Jehovah Witnesses built a new hall on Flier Drive next to the Cedars Subdivision in 1995.

The Pacific Church of Christ, which dates back to 1944, operated in the old Jehovah Witness building from 1991 until 2007, when the church constructed a beautiful new sanctuary and youth center at 112 North Payne Street.

First Christian Church of Pacific was organized in 1970 in the former B. F. Allen School building. In March 1987, First Christian Church purchased their current location at 422 West St. Louis Street from the Assembly of God Church. Rev. Jack Bone is the pastor.

In the 1990s, several new congregations began their own churches. Faith Fellowship Church opened on West Osage. The congregation later moved to 530 East Osage, where the congregation also operates a religious bookstore. Pastors Randall and Alice Pickens serve the church.

Mission Community Church began in 1995 with a few people meeting for Bible study in homes. The church purchased land on Highway N South of Old Gray Summit Road in Pacific with hopes to build in the future. Mission Community Church is a non-denominational Christian Church. The pastor is David Lange.

The New Beginnings Lutheran Church built a 6,000-square-foot building on the I-44 North Service Road in Pacific in 2007. The sanctuary seats 244 and the building includes office space and an assembly hall. Pastor Joe Sullivan started the New Beginnings Church in his Eureka living room in 1998.

New Apostolic Church, organized in 1999, now holds services in the West Osage Plaza at 2712 West Osage. Juergen Bloch is the minister.

Heart of Worship Community Church, at 2314 West Osage, is Pacific's newest church. Minister Tim Reeves and his wife Jennifer founded the church.

Bringing the tradition of the early churches full circle, sharing faith continues in Pacific to this day. For the past seventeen years, the Pacific Kiwanis Club has held an annual non-denominational Christian Prayer Breakfast at the Pacific Eagles building. In 2007, Jay Newman and his two brothers, John and Joe, began the tradition of sharing the Jewish Passover Seder with Gentiles in The Great Pacific Coffee Company dining room.

Tucked into a heavily wooded hillside on North Orr Street, the Pacific City Cemetery dates back to 1850. Today, local Boy Scouts place flags at the graves of veterans on Memorial Day. A Cemetery Committee oversees the maintenance of the cemetery, raising funds to repair historic stones, paint the wrought iron fence, and erect signs on city roadways directing motorists to the cemetery. The group has also built a spacious gazebo as a place for those visiting the cemetery to rest.

St. Bridget Cemetery, also located on North Orr opposite the Pacific City Cemetery, is owned and maintained by St. Bridget of Kildare parish.

Sunset Cemetery, situated immediately south of St. Bridget Cemetery, is privately owned.

Resurrection Hill Cemetery occupies a little knoll on Highway OO, north of I-44. This small cemetery also dates to the 1800s. The oldest recorded burial appears to be Jasper Wagner in October of 1895. It is not known whether he died elsewhere and was moved to this site or whether African American families were using the burial grounds prior to the time the city purchased the property and established

Pacific City Cemetery and St. Bridget Catholic Cemetery beyond the fence are located on North Orr Street.

Resurrection Hill Cemetery, originally designated for African Americans, dates to the 1800s.

the Resurrection Hill Cemetery for Colored People in 1909. Many graves in the cemetery do not have markers, but it is believed that the city cemetery sexton has records of who is buried in each gravesite.

PACIFIC *Care* CENTER

For more than twenty years, Pacific residents have enjoyed the convenience of long-term health care within the community. To make Pacific Care Center a reality would require a trip to the U.S. Supreme Court.

In 1980, Pacific citizens were invited to a public meeting at the Pacific High School Annex to discuss the lack of long-term health care in the city. Residents had to travel to neighboring communities to visit loved ones in nursing homes.

Mr. Al Brundick stood to say that his wife had been in a nursing home in Washington for ten years and he had traveled the forty miles each day to be with her and help with her care. Other residents spoke of the need for the city to care for its own elderly in the community. But not everyone was in favor of a nursing facility in Pacific. Representatives from area nursing homes, who feared a new home would be competition, spoke against the idea.

When Joe Dailey learned that the Dr. George Leber farm was to be sold, he and fourteen other residents formed a company to construct the Pacific Care Center. They were Joe Dailey, Ollie Preiss, Jack Grimm, Fred Hoven, Ralph Buscher, Garland "Ick" Noonan, Harold Goebel, Robert Schneider, Pete Hoffman, Helen Dailey Murray, Ed Buscher, Margaret Wahl, Art Muehler, and Bob Schmidt.

The partners not only wanted to build a care center in Pacific, they also wanted to accept Medicaid payment for individuals who could not afford long-term care. The other nursing homes in the area did not accept Medicaid and opposed a new care center that did.

Pacific Care Center.

Assisted Living.

When they presented a Certificate of Need to the State to build a center in Pacific, the application was denied. They sought relief in the district court and were again denied. They appealed to the State Appeals Court and were denied. Then, they appealed to the State Supreme Court, where their request was granted along with a ruling that nursing homes would be required to accept Medicaid patients. Opponents appealed that decision to the U.S. Supreme Court, which refused to consider the case, thereby allowing the Missouri Supreme Court ruling to stand.

On January 3, 1985, the state granted the permit. The first patients were accepted in 1986.

Today, Pacific Care Center is a skilled nursing facility with twenty-four-hour nursing service, licensed for 140 residents. The adjoining assisted living facility is licensed for sixteen residents.

The Pacific Care Center employs approximately one hundred people. Some have been there from the day the center opened. True to its commitment to care for Pacific's elderly in Pacific, the Care Center has provided a residence for several of the founding owners. Today, Mary Jane Labit, Dr. Leber's daughter, is a resident in the assisted living area.

Senior CENTER

$\mathcal{T}$he Tri-County Community Senior Center served its first meal on Sunday, April 15, 2007. Some 240 individuals signed the guest register during the grand opening celebration. The Pacific High jazz band entertained the gathering crowd for an hour, playing a medley of '50s-era tunes.

The Pacific High JROTC honor guard presented the colors to open the formal ceremony. Members of Girl Scout Troop 4263, Pacific, made their way among the senior citizens and dignitaries handing out butterfly sculptures and laminated bookmarks commemorating the grand opening. Senator John Griesheimer presented new U.S. and Missouri flags that had been flown over the state capitol to be displayed in the senior center dining room.

The center was built with $850,000 in combination with State Community Development Block Grant funds, state tax credits, and seven years of bake sales, quilt raffles, and other local fundraisers.

The lengthy fundraising effort was led by one feisty senior citizen: a retired federal worker named Helen Preiss. Often in failing health, Preiss attended the meetings of every civic organization in the community asking citizens to remember their parents and grandparents who had built the community. She wanted to build a senior center building that could never be taken away. Would they help her?

Preiss' building was the second-generation senior center. The Mid-East Area Agency on Aging (MEAAA) had operated a weekday meals program at the old American Legion building for thirty years from 1967 to 1997. When MEAAA closed the popular senior citizen gathering place and notified Pacific's elder citizens that they would have to drive to Eureka for meals, Preiss started her fundraising program.

Jeff Preiss logs onto the Internet in the senior center computer room as his mother, Jessie Preiss, looks on.

More than 400 individual contributions were received from churches, schools, businesses, civic groups, and individuals.

Jennifer Reed, who in 1999 was a member of a youth group, the Rainbow Girls, later named the Missouri Service Organization, was in the audience. The young women of that group had heard that Helen Preiss was raising funds to build a senior center in Pacific to replace the senior-meals program that had been taken to Eureka. The young women donated $500 toward the building.

"They were the first ones to believe in us and look where we are today," Ed Hillhouse, the senior center president, said.

Also present among the celebrants were Marie Buscher and Jessie Preiss, two members of the original committee that had created the Pacific senior center, bringing the senior-meals program to the American Legion hall forty years earlier.

Helen Preiss founded the center.

Before the doors opened, directors voted unanimously to name the building the Helen Preiss Building. Judith Gates is the senior center administrator.

In the end, MEAAA decided that it would not use the kitchen of the new building but would cater the meals from the Eureka senior center. The Tri-County Community Senior Center is the only center in Franklin County that has no government revenue stream. The center relies on fundraisers such as the twice-monthly jam sessions to raise operating funds.

Jam sessions serve as entertainment and as fundraisers for the senior center.

The Tri-County Community Senior Center, at 800 West Union, Pacific, began providing senior services on April 15, 2007.

AMERICAN *Legion* POST 320

*I*n May of 1920, a small group of World War I men led by Dr. J. W. Pletcher organized an American Legion Post in Pacific. The preliminary name, Colwell Harris, was chosen for the first soldier from Pacific killed in action during World War I. He was killed in Chateau-Thierry, France. Those signing the charter were G. Dewey Steinhaus, Charley O. Pfieffer, Charles W. Frieberg, Clifton A. Bowler, William Essman, Ulmont Krausch, G. Erwin Gross, J. W. Pletcher, Robert F. Ferrell, Frank C. Higgins, Dr. A. L. McNay, Samuel L. Jones, and L. P. Zitzman.

The first commander of the Post was Dr. A. L. McNay, who served in 1920. In 1923, Commander Gross organized an Auxiliary, but it soon disbanded.

The Post bought a lot in September 1930. After many years of hard work, the Legion home was built.

An Auxiliary was organized in 1939. Mrs. Blanch Pletcher was the first president. Those signing the charter were Blanch Pletcher, Therese C. Fischer, Evola B. Ryker, Edna J. Pritchett, Edith V. Howe, Mary F. Roberts, Mary Tobey, Maye Fallis, Minnie Stuck, Minnie McLaren, Helen Calvert, Wilma Bechtol, Ruby Savage, Edna Ridenhour, Dora Biller, Hattie Powell, Margaret Maupin, and Frances Kommer.

The first soldier from Pacific who was killed in action in World War II was Paul Williams. He died in September of 1943 in the Southwest Pacific. His name was then added to the official name of the Post, making it the Colwell Harris Paul Williams Post and Unit 320.

The Post home served as the center of cultural life in Pacific for decades and the building was the location of wedding receptions, public meetings, and banquets. The first Pacific senior center opened in the building in April 1967 and operated there for thirty years before it was moved to Eureka and the current Helen Preiss Building was constructed to house the Tri-County Community Senior Center.

The American Legion disposes of worn American flags in a flag-burning ceremony.

The frame building burned to the ground in a disastrous daylong fire in February of 2002. Firefighters from the West County, Boles, St. Clair, and Washington fire districts joined Pacific firefighters as citizens paced the sidewalks on Meramec and Fourth streets.

A new building was completed in 2006. Today, the Legion again offers its hall for rent and uses its kitchen for fundraisers to benefit the organizations it supports.

For thirty years, the Post 320 has sponsored a Legion baseball team. Two years ago, the Post joined the Adopt a Platoon Program, which sends mail and needed items to troops stationed away from home. It also holds periodic flag-burning ceremonies to properly dispose of worn American flags.

Post 320 is located at the corner of Fourth and Meramec streets.

Legion members march in the 2009 Sesquicentennial Parade.

The Post 320 officers are Ron Sansone, Post commander; Charles Young, first vice commander; Dave Monroe, second vice commander; Ed Tenny, adjutant/finance officer; Lloyd Borgstede, sergeant of arms; and Lynn Hess, historian.

The Auxiliary Unit 320 officers are Kathy Bay, president; Teresa Moore, vice president; Candy Cloak, secretary; Nancy Bush, treasurer; Mary Anne Borgstede, sergeant of arms; and Marlene Kaputska, chaplain.

The American Legion Post 320, at Fourth and Meramec, was built in 2006 to replace the original Post home that burned to the ground in February of 2002.

PACIFIC *Lions* CLUB

The International Lions Club was only nineteen years old when twenty Pacific men formed the Pacific Lions Club in 1931 to help their friends and neighbors whose lives were wrecked by the loss of jobs and lack of money to feed their families during the Great Depression.

The Lions raised enough money in their spare time to pay out-of-work men two dollars a day to work on civic improvement projects. They also provided food to destitute families and created a free breakfast program for area schoolchildren, long before the free breakfast programs that are taken for granted today.

Children were always on the minds of early Lions Club members. It was in 1937 that the club held an Easter egg hunt in Pacific for area children. The event proved to be so popular the tradition continued for the next sixty years.

They also looked to the adult needs of the community. One set of minutes in 1944 records that the club contributed $800 to the Volunteer Fire Department, one hundred dollars for repairs for the American Legion Post, twenty-five dollars for the Pacific Band, and with its remaining funds sent eighty-seven dollars' worth of cigarettes to local men in service.

In the 1960s, when the school started testing the vision of students, the Pacific Lions bought eyeglasses for Robertsville kids who needed glasses, starting the program that would be the club's mainstay to this day. The club raised funds, year after year, to provide eye exams and glasses for individuals who could not afford to pay for them.

In March of 2008, hundreds of visitors made their way to the Lions Den as the club loaned it to Service International, the organization that cleaned the south side of flood debris. Happy to see their building filled with traffic, the Lions also made a financial contribution to help the faith-based organization

Lions brave the cold to raise Christmas tree lights the first Saturday of December.

complete one of largest community service projects in the city's history.

Lions post flags in front of thirty local businesses every Memorial Day, Flag Day, Fourth of July, Labor Day, Columbus Day, and Veterans Day.

The Lions Club is probably best known in Pacific for the installation of the annual Christmas tree atop the bluff in Blackburn Park. In this era, the tree is a series of Christmas lights strung Maypole-fashion from a tall pole. Each year, the members take the box of lights to the top of the bluff, plug each string in to see which lights still work, and attach one end to the top of the pole.

Originally the Christmas trees were live, cut by the Lions and hauled up to the top of the bluff. They were allowed to go into Little Ireland, near St. Joseph's Hill Infirmary, and cut the largest tree they could find. When they brought it back to Pacific, groups of people would be waiting on street corners to see the huge tree go by. The arrival of the big tree always marked the beginning of the Christmas season. Residents recall that on the evening the tree was lit, people would gather at the foot of the bluff to sing Christmas carols.

The Lions Club 2009–2010 officers were Gary Wamsley, president; Don Brandt, first vice president; Brad Reed, second vice president; Tom Noonan, third vice president; Rose Ryder, secretary; Paula Stallings, lion tamer; and John Stallings, tail twister. Directors were immediate past president John Knoesel, Henry Hahn, Ron Sansone, Justin Mitchell, Myrna Pittman, and Dr. Ted Vargas.

The Lions Club building is located at Fourth and Meramec.

History MUSEUM

$\mathcal{T}$he Meramec Valley Historical Museum officially began its new life on Saturday, September 16, 2007, when upwards of fifty well-wishers gathered for a ribbon-cutting ceremony in a circa-1950s structure that was once the home of William and Frances Wolf. The small museum now showcases exhibits of local history.

The museum seems small at approximately 2,000 square feet, but museum officers field a group of art and history volunteers to make the former-home-turned-museum work.

The all-volunteer decorator group sorted through the collection of artifacts and printed items that the City Historical Committee assembled over a period of five years. They assigned spaces for the first official exhibit in the former living room. A third former bedroom serves as a museum office and the kitchen remains as a kitchen and meeting place for museum staffers.

The garage houses a gallery of photographs and names of area veterans from wars that date back to the Mexican War.

"People have brought us a great deal of stuff," said Hilda Bandermann, museum president. Janet Daniel, Gray Summit historian and Meramec Valley Genealogy & Historical Society (MVG&HS) archivist, cataloged the items to go on display and provided information tags identifying dates and pertinent facts for each display item.

A teachers' sorority visits the museum's Veterans Hall of Fame during a recent tour of the facility.

Volunteers spent hours toting items into the display area, hanging photos and prints on walls, and polishing glassware. Volunteers raised enough funds to purchase a computer, printer, scanner, digital camera, and photo printer. This was exactly what former alderman Jeffrey Titter (later mayor) had envisioned when he started the City Historical Committee eight years earlier.

With a penchant for local history, Titter and his committee began accepting contributions of local history memorabilia.

After the museum opened, it became the home of much of the vast local history collection of Gray Summit family history archivist Janet Daniel.

Hilda Bandermann and her daughter Jeannie began a collection of names and stories of local veterans who served in every war. When the American Legion Auxiliary rebuilt the downtown honor roll, they donated the former name board, containing the names of World War I and World War II veterans. Photos and stories poured into the museum, some left with no return address identifying the donor. The materials have been assembled in a Veterans Hall of Fame in the former garage of the building.

The museum is open to the public on Saturdays and Sundays from 1:00 p.m. to 4:00 p.m., and on Wednesdays from 10:00 a.m. to 2:00 p.m. ✍

Jeffrey Titter, former mayor, established the City Historical Museum.

A ribbon-cutting officially opened the history museum.

EAGLES *Aerie* 3842

$\mathcal{T}$he Fraternal Order of Eagles was founded in Seattle, Washington, in 1898 as an international non-profit organization, united fraternally in the spirit of liberty, truth, justice, and equality, to make human life more desirable by lessening its ills, and by promoting peace, prosperity, gladness, and hope.

The Pacific Eagles Aerie 3842 and its Auxiliary were formed on November 26, 1978, with eighty charter members. Marvin Gesemann was the organizer.

The Aerie started meetings at the Catawissa Veterans of Foreign Wars for about six months. They then met just for a couple of meetings at the American Legion, then at a factory at Columbus and Union streets, and then settled in at the Quonset hut on Osage Street. Later, they moved to the plaza on East Osage.

In 1987, the Eagles purchased the property at 707 W. Congress Street from the Union Pacific Railroad and completed the building of their current building in 1989.

The Pacific Aerie currently has 528 members and the Ladies Auxiliary has 241 members.

The Eagles Aerie and Auxiliary support numerous local and national non-profit organizations and charities. The following is a list of some of the organizations and charities that they are currently supporting: Eagles Alzheimer's Fund, Eagles MO-Kansas Bar H Boys Ranch, Eagles Art Ehrlmann

The Chamber of Commerce holds its annual Fantasy Night fundraiser in the Eagles' big hall.

Cancer Fund, Eagles Diabetes Research Center Fund, Eagles Robert W. Hanson Diabetes Fund, Eagles Max Baer Heart Fund, Eagles Jimmy Durante Children Fund, Eagles D. D. Dunlap Kidney Fund, Eagles Lupus Fund, Prevention of

Eagles Aerie 3842 Officers: Past Worthy President Robert McDermott, Worthy President Jim Agee Jr., Worthy Vice President Mike Noe, Worthy Secretary Jerry Eversmeyer, Worthy Chaplain Jim Agee Sr., Worthy Inside Guard Tom Weber, Worthy Conductor Joey Schaffer, Worthy Trustee Ron Pursley, Worthy Trustee John Casey, Worthy Trustee Mike Hawkins, Worthy Trustee John Welch, Worthy Trustee John Prince

Eagles Auxiliary Officers: Madam Past President Stacey Burden, Madam President Penny Morgan, Madam Vice President Kim Noe, Madam Secretary Mary Sokeland, Madam Chaplain Carol Finn, Madam Treasurer Leona Hodges, Madam Conductor Peggy McDermott, Madam Inside Guard Betty McCormick, Madam Trustee Peggy McIntyre, Madam Trustee Jackie Martin, Madam Trustee Mary Lou Neier

Child Abuse, Lew Reed Spinal Cord Injury Fund, Eagles Disaster Relief Fund, Breast Cancer Fund, Colon Cancer Fund, Red Cross, MO Boy State Program, Pacific High School Project Graduation, Dan Donnelly Backpack Fund, T-ball Team, Pacific Chamber of Commerce, Pacific Kiwanis, City of Pacific Fireworks Display, Meramec Valley R-III Teachers Association, Pacific Soccer Association, PHS USMC ROTC, YMCA Summer Camp supporters, Pacific Youth Association, local Boy Scouts, Pacific Sports Club, and many other benefits, dinners, and auctions.

The Eagles building not only serves as a meeting/social place for Eagles; with its large size of 25,000 square feet, it hosts a large meeting room, small hall, and a large hall. This building has served the area as a place where people can hold meetings, weddings, benefits, and auctions; it is the community center for virtually the entire Meramec Valley area.

Eagles Aerie 3842, located at 700 West Congress Street.

ORGANIZATONS &
Community
EVENTS

*P*acific public spectacles date back to a buggy ride to the river's edge to witness an imperiled introduction of steamboat travel on the Meramec River, which had all the amenities of a county fair. Later generations of outdoor events have included car shows, chainsaw carving contests, Mardi Gras parades, and a visit from the Moving Wall. They all bring the citizens out.

The first group of citizens to band together for mutual fellowship was the Freemasons A.F. of M. Pacific Lodge No. 159, chartered in April of 1856. William Inks, Thomas Watson, Louis Mauthe, and Albert Koppitz were among the members. Two years later, in September of 1858, the Franklin Lodge V.O.T.B. Unabhangizer Orden Des Truen Buendes Nummer 12 (the True Independent Order of True Union No. 12) was formed with Christ Alt, Hans Howe, Geo. Jahraus, William Knobel, Albert Koppitz, Lorenz Leber, Fred Mayle, Nicholas Rau, Louis Roemer, Edward Straumann, and George Zitzman among the members.

In 1885, eight men formed the Lodge Hargard Musical Group.

In 1892, the International Order of Good Templars Pacific Lodge was organized with eighteen members. In 1894, the Modern Woodmen Camp No. 582 was organized, and in 1897, the Royal Neighbors No. 615 came into being. That same year, the ladies organized the Valentine Lodge No. 81, Sisters of Ancient Order of United Workmen, with fifteen members.

In 1901, L. M. Goode, an African American citizen of Pacific, joined the Ancient Order of Free & Accepted Masons colored headquarters at St. Clair.

Eastern Star No. 129, with 141 members, was organized in 1915.

That same year, the Father Edward Berry Council 1335 of the Knights of Columbus was organized. Among the members were the leaders of the Irish community in Little Ireland—among the earliest settlers of the region—D. A.

Brennan, James P., Peter and John Dailey, L. P. McHugh, Edward Gross, William McKeever, J. McNamee, and James Phelan.

In 1914, Pacific was the chosen site for the Third Annual Frisco Travelers Convention—a gathering of the salesmen and drummers who rode the Frisco offering their wares to local merchants in Pacific, St. James, Springfield, and Santa Fe.

Whiskey bottlers, local brewers, dry goods manufacturers, and multi-story St. Louis hotel owners took ads in the ten-by-fourteen-inch printed program saluting their friends, the drummers. The organization had a board of directors and officers. The convention program listed twenty-one committees that would guide convention activities: registration, publicity, badges, baseball, entertainment, and dancing.

The Pacific Businessmen's Club followed suit and set up its own committees to welcome and entertain the visitors. The general arrangement committee was a "who's who" of Pacific leaders: G. C. Rau, G. A. Scott, L. P. Brennan, J. Z. Smith, E. A. Roemer, William Gross, and John J. Mauthe.

Antique cars line Union Street for the 2007 Cruise Night in Old Town Pacific. Some 650 pre-1985 cars registered for the event where the only prize is a bragging-rights trophy.

A salute to men and women in military service always brings Pacific residents out. Thousands of local citizens and visitors from nearby towns walked past the Moving Wall when the replica of the National Vietnam Memorial visited the city in 2008.

The Businessmen's Club would later become the Pacific Area Chamber of Commerce, which organizes events for children, college-bound co-eds, other civic organizations, and area businesses. In 2000, the Chamber introduced Spookfest in the city park as a safe trick-or-treat venue for families with young children. The event was a smash hit the first year, attracting thousands of visitors from the area. It continues to grow each year.

Fantasy Night, another Chamber event, enables one lucky participant to win $10,000 and pumped more than $200,000 into the local economy in its first five years.

The Chamber also holds an annual Queen Scholarship Banquet, which provides college scholarships for Pacific High School graduates. Scholarship recipient selection concludes with an evening gown presentation and a gala banquet.

The town held a 1918 Liberty Bond Parade.

In recent years, the Chamber introduced a "Made in Pacific" Exposition, where local manufacturers exhibited their products.

In 1920, after World War I, American Legion Post 320 was formed. The Post became the center of jitney dances and carnivals as Legionnaires tried to raise funds to build a Post home. They constructed a pavilion that still stands and constructed the Post home, a frame building that was the site of wedding receptions and other banquets for years and also served as the home of the first Pacific senior center.

The Pacific Chamber of Commerce conducts an annual Queen Scholarship contest for Pacific High graduates. Above, Queen contestants pose after the selection of the 2005 scholarship winners.

After World War II, the Legion Auxiliary raised funds for an honor roll, which was constructed at Second and Union streets. The names of soldiers were placed on a menu board, like a theater marquee. In 2007, the Auxiliary completely restored the monument, carving the dedication in granite. They held a dedication ceremony that filled the streets near the monument.

In the middle of the Great Depression, a group of local men formed a chapter of the new Lions Club. As a community event, the Lions created a gigantic Easter egg hunt that continued for decades. For decades, the street between the American Legion and the Lions Den was the site of an annual circus. Two years ago, the Lions revived the practice of bringing the circus to town.

As Pacific moved into the modern era, a group of white-gloved ladies began to hold monthly meetings, gather at vacant patches of land to plant flowers, and lobby the city fathers to dress up the city entrance and establish a permanent park system. The members of the Pacific Garden Club braved the mahogany-paneled offices of the Missouri Pacific Railroad in downtown St. Louis to demand that the railroad clean up debris along the tracks within the city. They encouraged the city fathers to create zoning districts dictating what could be built where and to establish a zoning board to regulate the districts.

But it was the flowers and parks that distinguished the Garden Club. In recent years, they have worked with businesses to line downtown streets with baskets of flowers.

LaVerne Wiest, wife of former mayor Bill Wiest, member of the Pacific Garden Club, and one of the charter members of the Pacific Park Board, was honored for beautifying the city.

The Garden Club works with area businesses to decorate sidewalks with baskets of flowers.

The Meramec Valley Genealogical & Historical Society was formed in 1970 to preserve local history and help families with genealogy. The organization is headquartered at Scenic Regional Library, 119 West St. Louis Street. The society maintains a local history and family history archive, which is housed at the Scenic Regional Library. The material cannot be removed from the library but is open to the public.

The 1970s also brought a flurry of activity from the Pacific Jaycees. In 2009, the thirty-eight members, ages twenty-one to forty-one, were working to improve the little league field at Riverbend School and provide a permanent scoreboard and bleachers. The club meets the fourth Monday of each month at The Great Pacific Coffee Company.

Eagles Aerie 3842 and Auxiliary at 707 West Congress is the location of many of the city's larger events. The organization supports scores of community charities.

The Eagles operate their own building, which includes a bar, a kitchen capable of providing meals for as many as 300 individuals, and offers three halls for public events. The Eagles' big hall is the site of the Queen Scholarship Banquet, annual Indians Sports Club Banquet, and Fantasy Night. The Eagles and Auxiliary support upwards of fifty different charitable groups.

In 1993, retiree Cleta Null organized the annual Adopt a Family Program that provides Christmas baskets to local families. Working with the Agape House Food Pantry and the Meramec Valley R-III School District, the program provides complete holiday meals, clothing, and gifts for area families in need. The first year Null provided for fifty families, giving the kids used clothing and toys. As the program grew, the school district began distributing applications to families in need of assistance. Today, each child receives new clothing and toys.

In the past sixteen years, Adopt a Family has served 643 families and over 2,300 kids at Christmas. In 2008, Cleta Null was named Chamber of Commerce Citizen of the Year.

The Pacific Partnership was formed in 2002 with a mission to revitalize Old Town Pacific, develop Pacific Station Plaza as a park, improve the appearance of Old Town, and attract new businesses. The Partnership would

Citizens stand in respectful silence for a ceremony rededicating the Soldiers' Memorial, which the American Legion Post 320 Auxiliary built in the city's first recorded park space at Union and Second streets.

Fantasy Night at the Eagles.

Children of all ages dress up in costumes to entertain families in a safe trick-or-treat venue.

later invite the other civic groups to form a coalition and combine resources and volunteers and was soon staging events that would attract crowds into downtown Pacific not seen since the day World War II ended.

Sgt. Dan Donnelly was recognized by the East West Gateway Council of Governments for his school supplies program.

The first downtown Cruise Night occurred in 2003, when the Tri-County Early Iron Club approached the city, the Chamber of Commerce, and the Partnership about moving its traditional yearly car show from the city park to the streets of downtown. Car Club members advertised the event among other clubs in the region, and on the day of the event registered some 400 cars. But nothing prepared the Partnership for the size of the crowd that filled the streets. Vendors sold out of food and the visitors poured into local businesses to use restrooms. Partnership organizers vowed that would not happen again, and they began serious planning for services and traffic control. Boy Scout Troop 329 agreed to help with clean-up after the event. The Pacific High School JROTC agreed to man entry checkpoints to prevent vehicles from driving into the Cruise Night area.

The Pacific Police Department stepped up its crowd control, bringing in all off-duty officers. The Pacific Fire District and Meramec Ambulance District placed vehicles and personnel in the area to be available for any emergency. Local businesses contributed thousands of dollars to provide restrooms and entertainment.

Patrons fill Second Street midway, where vendors' booths provide refreshments during the annual Cruise Night, organized by the Pacific Partnership and the Tri-County Early Iron Car Club.

Antique cars line St. Louis Street for annual Cruise Night.

In 2005, when Governor Bob Holden attended the event, the crowd was estimated at 20,000. Holden, who was running for re-election, was promised a crowd. When he stepped out of the limousine amid a sea of people he was overwhelmed.

As the community events flourished, Pacific Station Plaza, the little downtown park, began to take shape. The Burlington Northern Santa Fe Railway (BNSF) donated a caboose. A group of volunteers constructed a pavilion where visitors could sit and watch the eighty or ninety trains that pass through the city each day.

The Partnership used its skills at attracting crowds and providing the services to help stage a national chainsaw carving contest at Pacific Station Plaza for local artist Laura Reichert, which attracted carvers from across the U.S. The event raised $56,000 for the Children's Miracle Network.

The Partnership also helped to organize the Bluegrass Festival for Dee Walton and Michelle Bastean and added The Great Pacific Barbecue —a Kansas City-sanctioned barbecue cook-off—to its list of annual events. Soon the annual Railroad Day celebration and Christmas on the Plaza were added to the Partnership agenda.

The 2007 chainsaw carving competition raised $56,000 for the Children's Miracle Network.

Floats turn onto St. Louis Street during the 2007 parade.

Patrons lean into the wind as they await the Mardi Gras parade.

A little Mardi Gras queen shows her mask in 2007.

All public events are not so well manned. In 2007, a small group of volunteers organized an alcohol-free, family-oriented Mardi Gras parade in Old Town Pacific. No one could have predicted the number of entries that wanted to join the parade or the number who came to see it. The successful event was abandoned after the second year because of the unpredictable weather during Mardi Gras.

But as Mardi Gras was being considered as too harsh for the children it was designed for, another activity was captivating the community. A local police officer and his wife used $2,000 of their own funds to buy school supplies for area children who went to school without pencils and notebooks. They bought a backpack for each of the young students. The Pacific Eagles told Sgt. Dan Donnelly that they wanted to raise funds so he could provide more backpacks. Soon other organizations came forward, offering to hold fundraisers. The program grew from eighty children who received supplies the first year to more than 400 in 2009.

Sheila Steelman, Pacific community and economic development director, organized the first Railroad Day. The highlight of the day was a stop by Frisco Engine 1522, which had formerly made the passenger run through Pacific.

Santa entertains youngsters during the annual Christmas on the Plaza in 2008.

Carolers celebrate the season during Christmas on the Plaza.

The community turned out for the first Railroad Day in 2002.

Jim Schwinkendorf, retired BNSF executive in charge of steam excursions, had made his home in Pacific to be near the 1522, which a group of railroad enthusiasts ran on occasional junkets, but the September 2002 excursion was to be the final trip for the 1522 before it was retired permanently. Schwinkendorf and Steelman arranged for the old steam train to stop at a site near its old water tank on South First Street during the Railroad Day celebration.

An offshoot of the Pacific Partnership came to life when Jim McHugh originated the Pacific Ring Initiative to study sustainable environment and economy. McHugh penciled a fourteen-mile-wide circle with Pacific at the center as a model for sustaining air and water quality during a period of economic growth. With assistance from the University of Missouri, the Ring met at The Great Pacific Coffee Company and conducted studies on water quality, flood mitigation, alternative fuel, hillside development, and returning Amtrak passenger rail service to the city.

On the first Saturday in December, the Partnership closes out the year's activities with Christmas on the Plaza, an event that brings Santa Claus to town and officially opens the Christmas season.

Firemen raise a large American flag for the Railroad Day crowd.

Mounted Lancers, a clown, and a Red Roadster parade past the judges during the May 2, 2009 Community Parade celebrating the city's sesquicentennial year.

Pacific PROFILES

*P*acific is a city of fourth-generation families and newcomers migrating west to find space and amenities. Its fortunes have often been driven by its location on the river, the railroad lines, Route 66, and Interstate 44. The people who came here built a permanent destination, giving Pacific its dot on the map. Here is a collection of a few of their passions and persistence, skills and generosity, and their determination to complete a task.

William C. Inks, *Pacific Founder*
Within weeks after the start of the Civil War, William Inks, Pacific's postmaster, organized a Home Guard unit to protect the Pacific Railroad bridges. Inks was the unofficial founder of the City of Pacific, having platted a farm he purchased at the junction of the Pacific Railroad and its Southwest Branch. He called the new city Franklin but the name was later changed to Pacific, in honor of the recently arrived railroad. He was among a group of men who started the first school district, which evolved into the present-day Meramec Valley R-III School District. Fifty years after the war ended, a grand celebration in Stovall Grove honored Inks and the surviving veterans of his Home Guard unit. He is buried in a family cemetery in Allenton.

King William Adams, *Soft-Spoken Patriot*
In 1864, King William Adams and his wife were freed from slavery. At some point they settled in Pacific, where they raised ten children in a small stone building that had once been occupied by chickens. An unabashed patriot, Adams named his first son John Quincy Adams. He made a living doing yard work for well-to-do Pacific families. When not working, he always wore a suit, tie, and pressed white shirt. A non-stop talker, he taught his children and grandchildren to speak the clear language of their white neighbors, telling the children that if they respected themselves, they would be respected by others. It is a pattern that has carried through four generations to present-day Herbert Adams, his great-grandson,

who would spend his entire adult life in city government. He purchased a lot on South First Street for the construction of the First Baptist Church, which survived him by seventy-five years. His great-great-granddaughter, Rosalind Jordan, operates a daycare service in the building. She speaks in the same soft, modulated voice that is a family trademark. Adams is buried in Resurrection Hill Cemetery.

Robert M. Peck, *Railroad Bridge Builder*

Robert M. Peck came to Pacific in 1870 as director of bridges and buildings for the Pacific Railroad to place his office at the junction of the Pacific and Frisco railroads. He had been a gunboat builder for the Union Army during the Civil War when he was hired to take charge of the building of railroad bridges. At Pacific, he built a turntable and roundhouse for engine repair that the two railroads would share, a machine shop, and bridge works, which employed 1,000 men. In the Pacific shops, the men under his supervision built and maintained 1.4 million linear feet of bridges, an untold number of trusses, columns, and buttress bridges. He was said to be the highest paid executive in the Pacific Railroad system. Peck lived in Pacific for almost thirty years, traveling in his own private car. He is buried beside his wife in a section of the City Cemetery that was once a private cemetery on his property.

McHugh & Dailey, *Merchants*

In 1907, Lawrence P. McHugh and his brother-in-law, James J. Dailey, constructed the McHugh-Dailey Mercantile Emporium at Third and Orleans streets. McHugh and his wife, Helen, would have six children, while Dailey and his wife would have eight. The two families created living quarters on the second floor of the building and operated an opera house on the clear-span third floor that also served as the meeting place for the town board and the site of high school graduations.

Charles Clay Close, *Boom Town Promoter*

Charles Clay Close may have been the first Pacific businessman to take advantage of the real estate boom that followed the arrival of the railroad. He founded an insurance agency and real estate agency, served as publisher of the *Transcript*, the local newspaper, and served on several boards and agencies. He built a fine two-story home on the corner of St. Louis Street and Third Street, where Pacific Food now stands. In the newspaper, he complimented himself on his dandy appearance and for cleaning the streets in front of his house. He also advertised that he bought arrowheads and other Indian artifacts, amassing what was reported as the largest private collection of Indian artifacts in the state. Both his insurance agency and his arrowhead collection survived him. His daughter, Blanch, operated the business after his death until she sold it to Garland "Ick" and Laura Noonan. The Noonans sold the agency to Joe Bosse. The *C* in Bosse's NEC Insurance identifies the Close Agency, making it arguably the oldest business still operating in the city. His great-grandson, Greg Myers, inherited the core of his arrowhead collection.

Walter Leezy, *The Winningest Coach*

In the decade between 1920 and 1929, Walter T. Leezy, Pacific High principal and coach, guided his young athletes to an astounding number of silver cups and ribbons. In 1920, the Franklin County Athletic Association included girls in track and field events for the first time and Leezy's female athletes would dominate county sports. Three sisters, Catherine, Anna, and Irene Maguire, won regional and state meets, capturing the attention of St. Louis and national sportswriters. Leezy urged Catherine to choose one sport in which to compete. When she chose the high jump, he dug a pit on the school grounds and filled it with sand, creating a landing spot for her practice. In 1923, the boys' track and field team won the prestigious Frisco Traveling Cup for the third straight year, earning the right to display it in Pacific. In local newspapers, Leezy credited the win to Leroy Alt, his star runner who broke all mile records in the county.

Catherine "Kay" Maguire (later Horsfall), *Olympic High Jumper*

In 1928, Catherine Maguire wrote home from Amsterdam, where she was competing in the Olympic games as a high jumper, that she and the other American athletes were living on the ship and she had met a boy, who was "very nice." Catherine and her sisters, Anna and Irene, had been a power group in Franklin County track and field events ever since girls had been admitted to the games in 1920. Some claimed that their athletic prowess was the result of living on the south edge of town and having to walk three miles to school every day. Catherine's triumphant trip home from Amsterdam included a stop in New York, where Mayor Jimmy Walker gave her a key to the city, and a stop in St. Louis, where the St. Louis mayor held a huge parade. In Pacific, the town held a grand celebration at Pacific High School. She gave occasional interviews until her death in 1991.

Jesse Adams, *Power of the Written Word*

Jesse Adams was the first African American man to buy a home in Pacific. A prolific talker, like his father, King William, he went to real estate broker C. C. Close to help him become a property owner. He and his wife, Lillian nee Garrison, would raise seven children in that house. Jesse, who could never keep still, distinguished himself by reading the weekly newspaper to his neighbors and mitigating any disputes they had with each other or with local authorities. His daughter, Ella, who lived to age one hundred, helped to raise her younger brothers and sisters after her mother's death. King William Adams would die in Jesse's house with Ella and her cousin, Blanche, at this bedside. She would recall his final words: "Grandpa is going to leave you now. You girls be good."

Dr. John Pletcher, *Popular Dentist*

Dr. John Pletcher came to Pacific in 1904, just out of dental school. He embraced life in Pacific where he "supported every good cause." He was commissioned as a major in the Army Reserve Corps for his field hospital service in World

War I. He married the town belle, Blanch Close. He was active in the American Legion, the Freemasons, the Eastern Star, the Moolah Temple, and the State Dental Association. He served on the Pacific School Board and was friends with a former governor. He died from injuries suffered in an early morning fire when he lit the stove in his office. There was an explosion and Dr. Pletcher was burned over his entire body. He was taken to Missouri Baptist Hospital and died several hours later. The town was electrified with grief. The popular dentist was laid out at his home at Third and Union as was the custom of the time. The funeral service was to be held at the Presbyterian Church, but the crowd was so large it had to be moved to the Royal Theater, where mourners filled every available space. Those who could not get in stood—along the sidewalks on both sides of St. Louis Street—in respectful silence until the flag-draped coffin was carried out. According to a newspaper clipping reporting on his funeral, "it was probably the largest funeral that was ever held in Pacific." His son, Kenneth, in medical school at the time of his death, would later become U.S. Air Force surgeon general.

Blanch Close Pletcher, *Intrepid Organizer*

Blanch Pletcher could have been lost to history, sandwiched between a flamboyant father and a civic-minded husband and a U.S. Air Force surgeon general son, but she may have eclipsed all three in terms of local prominence. She operated her father's insurance business for forty years after his death, coming into contact with every youngster who reached driving age as the local notary public. When a polio epidemic claimed a large number of victims in Pacific, frightening the local populace into isolating the families, she donned a nurse's apron and cap with a red cross and visited the homes, helping with medical needs. She was a pillar of the Pacific Presbyterian Church.

Dailey Sisters, *Community-Minded*

The daughters of James J. Dailey would play their own roles in the life of Pacific, impacting education, tourism, and senior care. As the sisters grew up in the McHugh-Dailey Building, they were exposed to every element of public life, from entertainment to education to politics. As they became adults, they followed their parents' lead and looked to the betterment of the community. Three would become teachers at St. Bridget Catholic School. As members of the Queen's Daughters, they worked to purchase the statues and annually place the nativity scene on the bluff—a charming idea that captivated the community and earned it its place as a Route 66 tourist attraction, luring lines of cars from the St. Louis area each holiday season. Four of the sisters would participate in the five-year successful court battle that reached all the way to the U.S. Supreme Court, which brought the Pacific Care Center to the city. For decades, the local newspaper reported it when the sisters went out to lunch. Of the five sisters—Helen Dailey Murray, Marie Dailey Buscher, Margaret Dailey Wahl, Ann Dailey Noelker, and Rosemary Dailey Freeman—only the youngest, Ann and Rosemary, were surviving in 2009.

Kenneth Pletcher, *U.S. Air Force Surgeon General*

Lt. Gen. Kenneth Pletcher grew up in Pacific, the son of two of the town's most popular individuals, Dr. John Pletcher, a dentist, and Blanch Close Pletcher, daughter of Charles Clay "C. C." Close. He recalls that his mother had him reading *Beowulf* in elementary school, where his classmates became lifelong friends. After graduating from Washington University Medical School, he joined the U.S. Air Force. He was named surgeon general in 2005. He retired in Arizona with Musette, his wife of forty years. He was buried at Arlington National Cemetery with full military honors, where his son, Army Col. John Pletcher, accepted the flag from his coffin.

John Howe, *Daffodil Man*

Each spring, at the turn of the twenty-first century, Shaw Nature Reserve in Gray Summit announces the blooming season of its vast daffodil gardens and explains that the origin of the sea of white and yellow blossoms was John Howe, a local horticulturist who died in 1970. Howe, who never married, lived on a farm one-half mile north of the Pacific city limits. He grafted nut trees with such skill that they attracted the attention of international luminaries. University of Missouri horticulture classes came to observe his techniques. He took a three-year hiatus to Wyoming to study Shropshire sheep, which he brought to his hillside farm. His grapes won a certificate in the 1904 St. Louis World's Fair. But he would always be known locally as the daffodil man, who cultivated 300 varieties of daffodils, which he dug up each fall and filled in baskets that local gardeners could purchase for as little as one cent each. Many of his grafted nut trees and daffodils today survive him on his home place, Haue Valley Farm, which his grand-nephew, Bill McLaren, still maintains.

Joe McHugh, *Painter of Presidents*

In 1999, ninety-year-old Joe McHugh painted the face of President Bill Clinton at the bottom of a large multi-portrait of every U.S. president up to that time. He titled the work, started forty years earlier, "An Unfinished Portrait." He was the son of Lawrence P. McHugh, partner of James J. Dailey, who together built the McHugh-Dailey Building. In the building's heyday, young Joe romped the stairs of his three-story home, roller-skated on the third floor, watched a parade of public and artistic people flow through the building, and drew everything he saw. As the family moved away, leaving only him and his cousin, Joe Dailey, to man the flagship family edifice, he had the third-floor opera house all to himself as a painting and sculpture studio. Upon his death in 2005, a diaspora of his paintings, drawings, and sculptures was strewn among family members and acquaintances. Truman's marble bust is housed in the Truman Elementary Library. Lincoln's bust can be seen in The Great Pacific Coffee Company in the family building. His beautiful portrait of John Fitzgerald Kennedy is on the second floor. The two originals of his presidential portraits hang in the Franklin County Court House and Jefferson Community College.

Joe Dailey, *Man of Ideas*

According to his wife, Virginia, who survived him by ten years, Joe Dailey never threw away a piece of paper in his life. Among his notes and receipts she found a handwritten note to himself, penned in 1936. He was not going back to school (at St. Francis Borgia in Washington). The following year, he had second thoughts and enrolled in Pacific High and graduated with the first class in the new gymnasium in 1939—a year older than the other graduates. He would emerge as the patriarch of a far-flung Dailey clan and as half-owner with his cousin, Joe McHugh, of the building that bore their names. He would develop the city's first industrial park and was a leader in the development of Pacific Care Center. He delegated himself as the family spokesman, meeting occasionally with news reporters to relate the activities of his far-flung cousins, nieces, nephews, and grand-nieces and nephews. Today his sons, Tom and Mike, own the building with their cousins, Jim and Bill McHugh. Tom serves as president of the Care Center.

Udell Adams, *Stood for Tradition*

Udell Adams, Jesse's son, was a workaholic who founded a waste-hauling business and earned a contract with the city to pick up residential waste. Two stories tie Udell to Pacific history. In one event, the suggestion was made to rename Resurrection Hill Cemetery as the Martin Luther King Jr. Cemetery to honor the slain civil rights leader. Udell, who attended every Board of Aldermen meeting, stood to say that some things were traditional and should remain as they were. The name change was not made. In the second story, at the height of racial unrest in the country, a group of African Americans from St. Louis wanted to come to Pacific to form a protest. Udell met with them and told them that Pacific blacks did not experience their level of discrimination and did not want to protest. A non-stop talker like his father and grandfather, Udell had a talking relationship with many of his fellow townsmen, who described him as a gentleman—a man deserving respect. "You could always hear him coming," his son Herbert recalled, "because he whistled all the time. He was a wonderful whistler."

Garland "Ick" Noonan, *In the Game to Win 1922–1990*

Garland "Ick" Noonan is remembered as much for his competitive spirit in the games of baseball and softball as for the Pacific institutions he helped to develop. He graduated from Eureka High School, where he played baseball and basketball the year Eureka won the state basketball championship. He played minor league baseball for the Texas Rangers until World War II. He then served in the U.S. Army Air Force for twenty-three months in the Pacific Theater. After the war, he took a job at the Lincoln Mercury plant in Hazelwood and began playing baseball and softball for local teams. He met Laura Noonan following a baseball game in 1948. The couple married in 1949. They bought a Pacific insurance agency and became real estate brokers and appraisers.

Noonan was at or near the center of developing the Pacific Community Park, city swimming pool, Hawthorne Subdivision, and the Frisco Pacific Industrial Park, where twelve industrial buildings are now in operation. He was active in local politics and public issues.

In an ironic twist of fate, in 1976, he was diagnosed with Amyatrophic Lateral Sclerosis (ALS), or Lou Gherig's Disease. Vowing to live with it instead of die with it, he survived for fourteen years. He died on December 31, 1990. His wife, Laura, and son, Tom, continue to operate the Noonan appraisal business.

Elda Zitzman, *Educator*

Elda Zitzman was named elementary school principal when all twelve grades of Pacific Public School were still held in what is presently known as the Community School Building. Elda Zitzman Elementary School was named in honor of her contribution to local education.

A daughter of one of the oldest families in Pacific, Ms. Zitzman was born in the historic William C. Inks building at 120 West Osage, which her family acquired in 1890. She attended Pacific Public School and became a teacher in 1925 at a school south of Robertsville. She began teaching in Pacific in 1926.

She was named principal of the elementary school in 1940 but continued her own education, earning a master's degree in administration from Washington University in 1954. She retired in 1968.

Dr. Marple Agee, *School Administrator*

When the Meramec Valley Middle School moved into the new school on Indian Warpath Drive, the new building was named for Dr. Marple Agee, superintendent of the Meramec Valley R-III School District. Although he lived in Pacific a short time, Dr. Agee left a mark on the community. He served as school superintendent when the present district was Reorganized Franklin County School District R-III, was instrumental in aligning the district with the St. Louis Community College District, and accepted the Nike Missile Base, which houses Nike Elementary School and the district transportation department. He was a leader in the field of special education and started a work/study program to enable students to build work skills.

In 2009, his grandson, Matt, taught at Pacific High School and his daughter-in-law, Mary Clasby-Agee, served on the school board. His picture is on display in the entrance foyer of the building that bears his name.

Sue Reed, *Historian on Horseback*

In 2008, Sue Reed published her second local history book, an account of the Jeffries family in Franklin County, which she compiled over a thirty-year period of studying local history while serving as a Pacific librarian. She and her husband, Jim, live in a country house built with their own hands and crafted with, among other things, the windows of the demolished Pacific train depot. As a librarian, she clipped obituaries and stories on local residents from newspapers, which she sometimes stacked in boxes and file drawers in the library. These papers would become the core of the Meramec Valley Genealogical & Historical Society archive. Sue wrote her first book, *In Retrospect*, as part of the Franklin County sesquicentennial in 1968, and it became the accepted authority on local history. Through it all, she would have rather been on horseback. In failing health, she achieved a dream of riding with Jim in his Moolah Mounted Lancer jacket in the 2009 Pacific Sesquicentennial Parade.

Linda Wells, *Winning Coach*

Linda Wells recalls a childhood as an athlete who, instead of playing with dolls or going to the mall, was always looking for another ball game. At Pacific High, she played four sports, and in college, three sports. But as assistant coach at the University of Minnesota, she singled out women's fast pitch softball and forged a career that earned her the title, "one of the winningest softball coaches of all time." She coached at Arizona State University, leading the Sun Devils to seven regional championships and two trips to the Collegiate World Series. She would be asked to help build and coach the first Greek national softball team as an entry into the Olympic games when that country hosted the games in 2004. She also served as assistant coach to the Dutch national team in the 2008 Bejing Olympics. Her parents, David and Blanche, were on hand when the practice field in Pacific Community Park was named Linda Wells Field. Although she bought a retirement home in Pacific, she is still chasing that next game around the world, holding clinics, and speaking.

George Hinkle Jr., *Learned the Game*

George Hinkle Jr. was a country boy who never held a football in his hand until he entered Pacific High School. He would learn the game so well that he would earn a college football scholarship to the University of Arizona and be drafted to play professional football for the San Diego Chargers. After his professional football career, Hinkle returned to his Robertsville home and served on the Meramec Valley R-III School Board from April 2001 to April 2006. In 2007, he was named Pacific High head football coach, vowing to teach young men not only to play the game of football but also to be better men. He and his wife, Sharon, have two sons, George II and Jeffrey.

Jo Ann Hoehne, *Face of City Hall*

The one word most commonly used to describe City Clerk Jo Ann Hoehne, who retired on July 3, 2008, is that she is "nice." Soft-spoken and unfailingly polite, Hoehne had a reputation for returning phone calls, compiling esoteric lists, and having a thorough grasp of city ordinances, finances, and recent history. When confronted with something controversial, Hoehne would respond with her trademark exclamation, "Oh my cow!" Jo Ann Hoehne was the face of City Hall for twenty-seven years, serving under seven mayors (eight, if you count that Herbert Adams was re-elected after a term out of office). She served as city clerk and city administrator, both at the same time for a period. She served as a director of the Chamber of Commerce and the Tri-County Community Senior Center and was active in the Municipal League, where she made friends across the state. She and her husband, Bud, have relocated to their home in Shell Knob, Missouri, on Table Rock Lake.

Barbara Bruns, *Beautified the Cemeteries*

Barbara Brundick Bruns, who died in 2006, formed the City Cemetery Committee, which raised funds to restore damaged gravestones and the antique wrought iron fence, build visitor gazebos in the City Cemetery and Resurrection Hill Cemetery, and erect signs identifying the cemeteries. She and her husband, Harlan, lived on Brundick Lane, the street leading to her parents' home, and raised one son, Keith. It was her husband's family that had served for three generations as cemetery sextons, but the city lacked the funds to maintain the two beautiful cemeteries. She and her committee turned to the descendants of those buried there asking for contributions. The fundraising effort worked. Although she is buried in the Catholic Cemetery, across the road from the City Cemetery, her family erected signs reminding future generations of her work returning the aging cemeteries to their former beauty.

Lloyd Baker, *Pied Piper of Ice Street*

In 1962, Lloyd Baker noticed the steady stream of campers that stopped in Pacific on their way to the Lake of the Ozarks and opened Baker's Standard Service on West Osage near the I-44 exit ramp. He began to make ice in a small building beside his station, which he sold by the bag. In 1997, he constructed an ice plant that stretched half an acre under one roof and produced 200 tons of ice a day, making it three times the size of any other Missouri ice plant. In an unabashed flair of ego, he named the short thoroughfare leading to the plant "Ice Street." Baker spoke with a candid simplicity that could encourage his adult children and employees to respectful silence, but small children responded to his papa bear gruffness and he responded to them. Sami Pigg, his eight-year-old grand-daughter, called him Papa Ice and considered him her best friend. When he was hospitalized and gravely ill, Sami wrote a note to her classmates about his illness. "He's my mom's dad," she wrote. "I figured this out last night." This regard for the prospects of young people led Baker to organize and annually sponsor the Queen program that provides college scholarships for Pacific High seniors. He contributed to every local cause, prompting one local journalist to dub him the Pied Piper of Ice Street. Until his death in 2002, he and his wife, Mary Ellen, lived in Pacific. They had three children: Diana Carter, Jill Pigg, and Tim Baker.

Ed Gass, *Mr. Public Works*

In 2008, Ed Gass retired as City Public Works director after forty years of laying water lines and fixing leaks. As the city expanded its boundaries, he was called upon to add new territory to the City Water Works. He found he could do more by using city labor to install new lines, leading some critics to refer to his department as the Gass Construction Company. But as a city with little or no money, it could contract out but one job a year, or like families, use the do-it-yourself method to provide critical services. He hopped on a grader himself to level land donated for a city park. In retirement, he continued to serve as consultant to the city.

Ruth Muehler, *Accidental Genealogist*

Ruth Muehler became the unofficial genealogy arbiter after discovering the contents of a box of old letters in the attic of the farmhouse. She and her husband, Art, would help organize the Meramec Valley Genealogical & Historical Society, with Neil Brennan serving as the first president. Her zeal for family history inspired society members to help longtime librarian and history writer Sue Reed amass an archive on local families, but it was Ruth's prodigious memory of the interconnected families in the eclectic archive that helped amateur genealogists locate family records. She lives with her cat, Chip, on West Union Street, in the house that she and Art built and where they raised their two children, Keith and Mary.

James L. McHugh, *Centered Pacific*

In 2002, James L. McHugh stepped into Pacific history after inheriting one-fourth of the century-old McHugh-Dailey Building at South First and Orleans streets. He had worked for forty years as an attorney in St. Louis, headed political campaigns, and served on the University of Missouri Board of Curators. He and his wife, Patricia, live in Webster Groves, where his dentist father moved the family in 1930. In Pacific, he urged then-mayor Jill Pigg to form the Pacific Partnership to instigate the renewal of Old Town and talked his fellow owners—his brother, dentist Bill McHugh of Marthasville, and his cousin, Virginia Dailey—into resurrecting the deteriorating family building, returning it to its glory days as the center of cultural activity. Today, The Great Pacific Coffee Company, a folksy sandwich and coffee shop, operated by David McHugh, one of James and Patricia's four sons, occupies the first floor, which hosts bi-annual meetings of the Pacific Ring, another McHugh creation that placed Pacific at the center of a fourteen-mile-diameter area staked out for economic and environmental sustainability studies.

Bill McLaren, *Coalition Builder*

In 2002, Bill McLaren formed the Pacific Community Action Committee (PCAC), a coalition of civic groups. After years of hauling his steam engine barbecue pit to town each weekend and cooking for not-for-profit organization fundraisers only to find that a conflicting fundraiser on the same date had taken the hoped-for crowd, he thought that if all the groups coordinated their activities, everyone would benefit.

He made his PCAC a sub-committee of the Pacific Partnership and reached an agreement with the city for the PCAC to operate four public events: spring Pride Day, Cruise Night, Railroad Day, and Christmas on the Plaza. The work was so successful that McLaren and company were soon asked to help stage a Blue Grass Festival, an annual barbecue cook-off, and a chainsaw carving contest. On being elected Partnership president, he stepped up efforts to improve Pacific Station Plaza, a small park on South First Street, as a train-watching venue. As a grading business operator, he used his connections in the construction business to build a pavilion in the Plaza. He also maintains Haue Valley Farm, the homeplace of his uncle, the late horticulturist John Howe. He and his wife, Linda, have two daughters, Kristin and Kesha.

Ron Reed, *Life in Law Enforcement*

In 2006, Ron Reed was elected municipal judge after serving twenty-five years as Pacific police chief. He brought the department into the modern era, adapting to new technology and training requirements for officers. Through the years, he reminded aldermen that his department never went over budget. He and his wife, Marigene, combined his sons and her sons to create a family. A hands-on chief, he directed traffic at parades, funerals, and public events, carried victims on litters at accidents, and lobbied aldermen for funds necessary to operate a modern police department. As a member of the Pacific Eagles, he can always be found cooking at banquets and fundraising barbecues.

Herbert Adams, *Fourth-Generation Speaker*

Herbert Adams, the son of Udell and Marie Adams and great-grandson of King William Adams, was born in 1955. Adams said he began to feel the stirrings of community involvement in junior high school when a social studies teacher assigned news stories for students to read, required current event essays, and held weekly class discussions on news topics.

"I was always a good student, but that really clicked for me," Herb said. "I couldn't wait for the day we had the discussion."

He graduated from Pacific High in 1973 and attended Meramec Community College for two years. During high school and college, he began working in the family business, Adams and Son Waste Hauling. In 1986, he went to work for a local car dealer and would spend his entire adult career as a car sales manager. At age twenty-five, Adams was elected municipal judge, breaking two records. He was the youngest individual elected municipal judge in the city and the first African American municipal judge. He served as municipal judge until 1992, when he ran for mayor. He was the first African American mayor, serving one two-year term and one four-year term. He was defeated for re-election in 1998. In 2002, he was again elected municipal judge, and in 2006, he was elected mayor for a third term. Adams and his wife, Yolanda Hinkle Adams, have two daughters, Jocelyn and Danielle.

Bibliography

Anonymous. "Pacific Looking Backward," circa 1930.

Brundick, Ed. *Memoir: Growing up in a Railroad Town*. Pacific, MO:
Heritage Bookstall, 2000.

Burton, K. W. "A Short History and Biographical Sketch of Pacific,
Missouri," circa 1930.

Frisco Railroad. *History of the Frisco*. St. Louis, MO: 1965.

Iowa 3rd Brigade. "Report of Activities in Franklin, Missouri."
U.S. Army Archives, 1864.

Jeffries, Achilles. *Jeffries, Sifting Through Time*. Pacific, MO: Heritage Bookstall, 2008.

Kiel, Gottleib. *Centennial Biographical Directory of Franklin County, Missouri*.
Washington, MO: Republished by Missourian Publishing Co., 1986.

Missouri Bureau of Geology and Mines. *The Sand and Gravel Resources of Missouri*.
Rolla, MO: 1918.

Missouri Pacific Railroad. *History of the Missouri Pacific*. St. Louis, MO: 1965.

Reed, Sue. *In Retrospect*. Pacific, MO: 1980.

Schwinkendorf, Jim. "A Railroad Retrospective." Unpublished report.
Pacific, MO: 2008.

Index

About the

AUTHOR

*P*auline Masson is a career journalist who has been the Pacific editor for the *Washington Missourian* since 1997. She was awarded a citation from the California Assembly for a series of investigative reports on industrial arts education in the state. With her son, Joe Cotham, she founded and published *Building Services Journal*, a monthly trade tabloid newspaper, and briefly published *Franklin County Business*. She has written two previous books: *Restoring the Old Rock Church* and *Schools in the Meramec Valley*. She and her husband, Robert, a retired Ralston Purina executive, own Sand Mountain Books, a small press publishing company that has published fifteen local history books by eight different authors in the past five years, which are sold through area historical societies.